I0528875

Je M'Accuse...

LÉON BLOY

Translated By Richard Robinson

Sunny Lou Publishing Company
Portland, Oregon, USA
http://www.sunnyloupublishing.com

2nd Edition, Revised and Corrected: January 9, 2024
Original publication date: July 14, 2020

ISBN: 978-1-955392-51-8

This translation from French is based on the
Édition de "La Maison d'Art" of
Je M'Accuse..., Paris, 1900.

Contents

Introduction

> *Yes, without a doubt, Émile, I take it you suffer for being thought of, by young people, – perhaps, also by some old people like myself, – as a good-for-nothing nincompoop and senile old man. Your Venetian probity forced you, in 1896, to strum that guitar indecorously...*

Preliminary Declaration

> *Cloacam maximam, receptaculum omnium purgamentorum urbis (id est Zola), ...dicebat Patavinus.[1]*

This book should have appeared before the end of last year. No publisher, until now, dared publish it. This simple fact speaks volumes about what we have suffered.

So, there was only one voice in France to protest this universal debasement, and this voice lacked the means to make itself heard. Very well, it was better to wait, doubtless, until today to bellyache.

The Affair is distant, so terribly distant, that it has become telescopic. It has, by consequence, ceased to obstruct the little reason left us by the democratic filth.

Some furious men of last summer have seen their fury die down in the equitable contempt where all mimes of the atrocious farce have been drowned.

The imbeciles themselves begin today to catch

---

[1]*Cloacam... Patavinus*: Latin for "The greatest sewer, the receptacle of every piece of filth in the city (i.e., Zola), according to Patavinus."

a glimpse of the magnificence by which they have been mocked, and how much Zola has turned his back on Truth and Justice, whose vocables he dared pollute by his filthy hand.

The funny man, however, with his caruncle always in the wind and all his tail feathers in the air, does not seem to have lost one iota of importance.

Has there ever been anything so unprecedented, so inconceivable, so damning?

The nation of Châteaubriand, Lamartine, Victor Hugo, Balzac, prostrated before Émile Zola!!! And nobody vociferates, nobody fills heaven and earth with lamentations, at the spectacle of that frightful ignominy!...

I knew an artist, a true one, an exceptionally lofty and noble being, whom the very name of Zola offended, revolted, sent running, as only excrement could have done.[2]

Ah well! since the Affair, he has become the admirer, you have read that right, the ad-mi-rer of Zola, the very respectable servant of the titular of that name of vomit and opprobrium!

Having descended to the level of the filthy bourgeois, he firmly believed, as the lowest dog of the last resoler of shoes in Brussels or Grand Montrouge[3] might have believed, that the scribe of Rougon-Macquart was capable of a flash of disinterestedness or generosity...!

After this, how not to believe in the stultifying power attributed to certain demons?

_____
[2]an artist: Henry de Groux.

[3]Montrouge: a suburb in Paris.

As for myself, I declare that I would sooner expire under the most horrible of torments before being sacrificed to so fecal an idol, or even before consenting to look on him, were it only once, and from afar, without expressing, in one manner or another, my immense disgust.

Even if I were the only one, I would revile and I would shout down, until all my strength were gone, the repugnant cretin and abominable senile guttersnipe, adored for his villainy by craven sons of the Queen of vanquished nations.

If France is cursed, rejected by God, lying under people's feet, if that is really what must be expected, when she dies once and for all, and everything ends and the planet, deprived of its soul, rolls over, like a dead thing, in the immensity!...

No matter what, it would be better than this wallowing in the dejections of such a son of a bitch!

    – Léon Bloy
    Kolding, Denmark, Good Friday, April 30, 1900

To Octave MIRABEAU
celebrated contemner of false artists,
false great men, and false good ole boys.

JE M'ACCUSE[4]

very humbly and very sorrowfully for having, on
January 21, 1889, published in *Gil Blas*, a stupid article
wherein I prostituted the name of "Anteus" with respect
to Émile Zola, supposing this abortion of a man to possess – materially only, it is true – a greatness.

It was a thousand times too much, I confess, and
my repentance is sincere.

Doubtless, the excessive ignominy of his latest
works had not yet jumped out at me. But had there not
been enough of the earlier garbage?

To be honest, I am all the less to be excused as I
was having to deal with, *for the first and last time*, an
extremely precarious situation at the filthy journal that
employed me.

I put this out there so that my excellent
colleagues, who spend their lives pounding the
pavement, might know at what point I am just like them.

The role of the Ass in "Animals Sick with the
Plague"[5] pleased me immensely, and I will go along
with it willingly.

Maybe I might also obtain, in this way, the
silence of some redoubtable friends who do not miss
any opportunity to remind me, with biting eulogy, of
this misadventure that dishonors me.

– Léon Bloy

---

[4]*Je M'Accuse*: French for "I Accuse Myself" or "I Stand Accused."

[5]Animals... Plague: a story by Jean de La Fontaine.

Part the First

The Cretin of the Pyrenees

People are told to look on high. It is a manner of speaking that, sometimes, seems impious to me. – A discourse given by Zola at a banquet of students. May 18, 1893.

Work is something that saves us from dreams and chimera and assures us of health. – Idem.

The working man is always good. – Ibidem.

All the Romance-speaking countries take me for an honest worker. That is good enough for me. – Interview of the same by an imbecile at *"Gil Blas,"* March 26, 1894.

I am still rather strong, and young people almost never have a strong enough grip to sever the lions' *hamstring... As far as I am concerned, I have no great interest in departing.* – Same interview.

I.

I paid *two thousand four hundred francs* for the last novel by M. Émile Zola. That honest and good worker, who has no qualms about profiting by others' work, deigned to deduct, for a rather long period of time, thirty percent of my family's bread.

I invested myself with that distinguished decoration in my book: *Léon Bloy Before the Swine*, which I made, moreover, as seemed fitting, into the most overzealous homage to the old *lion* who reigns over, at Médan, Paul Alexis, in the vicinity of Poissy.

One will grant me, I daresay, that such a contribution gives me the right to speak, once again, about M. Zola, even if it were to flatten myself like a flea before the majesty of that money collector.

For about two years after the announcement of *Lourdes*, I had accumulated at home old journals mentioning diverse discussions by the high priest, from which I expected to draw a great amount of wisdom and knowledge. Alas!

"I ask myself sometimes, with a certain anxiety," – said, one day, to his dear students, the revealer of the *Religion of Work*, – "I ask myself what would become of my work in the hands of the young people whom I feel are coming up behind me." The response is too simple.

"My documents," I predict, "will indubitably be thrown into the latrines, together with the book of *Lourdes* itself, and I would gladly submit to having my ass boiled if I could find a more pertinent employment for them."

The brain of *Rougon-Macquart*'s creator, whatever its tonnage might be, does not contain a great variety of merchandise. When one has read one hundred lines of this literary merchant, one has read everything, and the crushing mass of his latest abortion adds absolutely nothing to the lack of balls that preceded it.

It is always, invariably, the coarse experimentalism of a side of Pork on the fixed menu, the horror of the mystery, the science, the evolution, the work, the holy coitus, the eternal return of atavism, heredity, degeneration, etc. And all that vileness of ideas, with what style, good God!

Ah! he does not try anything new, the old serpent, and hardly *evolves*, I assure you.

Zola's clichés are quite well known: "the sun that *puts its clear note* on something," for example. Although I have not counted them, I estimate that they can hardly surpass thirty or forty in number, served regularly and indefatigably, since the *Rougons* and the *Macquarts* have been in existence.

It appears that that suffices for the one hundred fifty thousand clients of *Nana* or the *Debacle*. Many others ought to find that it is still too literary, too encumbering.

The output would be perhaps more enormous if he wrote decidedly, resolutely, and completely like a police officer or border patrol officer, but something must be done for the Academy.

Each one of his indestructible clichés, which Monsieur Zola is the happy tenant of, were calculated for an indeterminate number of identical situations where the reader is always sure to find them. It is really difficult to exhaust oneself less than this great worker does.

I cannot be accused of fanaticism for Flaubert certainly, all whose books, with the exception of one, have exasperated me. Everyone, however, knows the

infinite labor of this man, "courageous like all lions,"
I said in 1890, in a funeral orison, – "but obsessed
with one imbecilic idea and forcing himself, for twenty years, to pull out of his intestines the seditious and
inextirpable tapeworm of his Inspiration."

Being nothing but a stubborn man, Flaubert
could not create a work of genius, but he was, incontestably, one of the most *upright* writers ever seen. He
left few books behind, because he himself was not
happy with them, if one can even say that he was happy, and these books, obtained with such great pain,
sold little, not being written for the multitude.

What would he say, the incorruptible Flaubert,
upon reading *Lourdes* or *Bête Humaine* today? while
seeing reappear, every twenty pages, the isochrone
formulas of this unconscious pendulum that one calls
the author and whose perpetual back and forth move-
ments would make an albatross seasick?

What would he bawl out using his *mouth-
piece*, that tempestuous martyr of the phrase, upon
learning that such an abject domestic of the populace,
such a messiah of the shit bucket and the ass wipe,
dares, sometimes, to mention him as a predecessor?

II.

"One comes away from a reading of *l'Assommoir* likes a pig leaving the mire. The mire, in effect:
a mire of things, a mire of words, an unrespirable
mire.

"M. Émile Zola has chosen to work exclusively in the Disgusting. We have learned from him that
one can delve considerably into human filth and that a
book made of that alone could have the pretension of

being beautiful...

"The author of *l'Assommoir* is a soiled Hercules who shovels the dung of the stables of Augeas and who adds his own to it! If you do not believe me, read his book. Plunge yourself into that sinkhole of excrement and if you can stay there without suffocating, or without vomiting, you will see that the filth there aspires to be even greater than art.

"M. Émile Zola believes that one can be a great artist in mire, as some are great artists in marble. His specialty, all his own, is mire. He thinks that he can be very like a Michelangelo of manure!...

"His language as an artist, – he has degraded it and lost it using the most ignominious slang of cabarets. He has chosen the language of the people. Depraved by his own subject, he speaks, in this book, like one of the characters that live in it. He makes use of a style that it is impossible to glean a phrase from, even if one had the pointed stick of a rag-and-bone man and the basket to throw it in. He no longer has a personality!

"He has forgotten Balzac, whom he imitated too much. That great man of the *Human Comedy* created and often spoke of, for the necessity of his novels, Auvergnats, Germans, porters; but he did it without becoming an Auvergnat, a German, or a porter. When the dialog ends, the novelist returns to his recitation and his page, pouring his style and his thought into it, but M. Zola has neither style nor thought to pour.

"He has nothing anymore in his belly than the conscience itself of his characters, than their ignoble passions, their horrible manners of feeling and expressing themselves. He has sunk and dissolved so deeply into their mud that he cannot lift himself up out of it enough to describe it. He has become mud just like them... A deserved castigation for a talent that has demeaned itself."[6]

It seemed agreeable to me to put before the eyes of the reader this piece by Barbey d'Aurevilly, written the day after *l'Assommoir* came out and which piece has probably been forgotten.

III.

Factory owners or general managers of grocery depots will with difficulty admit, I am quite sure of it, that a novelist who earns two or three hundred thousand francs a year from a single tome could be a *cretin*.

God help me from the temptation of attempting to make these useful men understand anything whatsoever; but I am ready to hand over my heart to the person who would reveal to me one word more just, one epithet more true, one qualificative more certain, one plaster more advantageous to harden the face of a scribe, already protected by the plastrons of glory, who has been unable to come up with one paltry idea in thirty years, a poorly clad idea that would veritably lend itself to him. It is confounding.

M. Zola is the Christopher Columbus, the Vasco de Gama, the Magellan, the great Albuquerque of the Commonplace. He equips a flotilla of three hundred ships and impresses a naval force of thirty thousand temerarious men to discover that "not ev-

---

[6]Original footnote: In response to this judgment by the great writer whose boots he was not worthy to shine, M. Zola did not fail to publish, peremptorily, that the author of *Les Diaboliques* was POOR.

erything in life is rosy," that "one is not young forever," or that "money does not make happiness."

"This continent is mine!" he shouted at that moment, while stamping his feet like a conqueror, and he deploys, in the name of Positivism, the bran-colored banner of documentaries.

The Commonplaces spurt out nonstop from this conquering Discoverer, like water from miraculous founts.

In the horrifyingly copious books that preceded the *trilogy* that we offer today the first song of, the commonplaces, always channeled according to some method, had flowed from diverse valleys of Love, Dreams, Politics, Debauchery, Art, High Wedding, High Commerce, Rustic Life, Finance, or War; because the yellow river had seemed to form into a delta, at uncountable mouths.

Lourdes, a religious subject, is the great estuary and the other arms of water seem like nothing at all anymore. Nothing short of the Pyrenees was needed to dump over us this torrent of philosophical and humanitarian dishwater.

"Blind faith, – obedience without examination, – total abandonment of reason, – faith that suffocates the torturing need for truth, – proven phenomena that demolish dogmas, – strict devotion, – the miracle by suggestion, – the *will to believe*, – the sadness of no longer believing, – divine ignorance, – the *devouring illusion* of divine love, – exaggerations!!! – happiness through faith that exists in ignorance and deception, – priests who are no longer men, – *castrated* priests, – *voluntary* suicide, the free and virile life on the outside"; etc., etc., etc.

I am telling you that he did not cross out a single one of them. All that can be vomited by the most

mediocre, most stupid, most ignorant, and most unclean among traveling salesmen or in the lowly anti-
clerical serialized novels edited for impious cobblers;
all the residue of old, fetid opinions, vomited former-
ly by renegades themselves, greedily slurped up again
by abominable prigs and vomited again in long
streams by the gob of the last dogs of Materialism; –
M. Zola has collected them like most-precious condi-
ments and thrown them by the handsful into his caul-
dron.

And phrases like these: "History never goes
backwards, humanity cannot return to its childhood. –
The inexplicable alone constitutes the miracle. –
What good is it to believe in dogmas? *is it not enough
to weep and to love?*"

In the end, there are six hundred pages of this!
To be honest, those accustomed to this cuisine can,
without noticeable waste, be satisfied reading by using a pair of scissors. As I said earlier, too many old
acquaintances are encountered there and even the pigs
get tired of never being thrown new pieces of excrement.

IV.

That my readers might pardon me for going
on so long about M. Zola whom it is no longer permitted to associate with literary concerns.

If it only had to do with a new publication by
this financier of the quill, my respect for Art would
have imposed on me a most profound silence. But the
superior attitude that this squat man assumes today,
from atop his ecus, – amassed a bit too cynically from
the possessions of the poor, – seems to me very close

to becoming completely unsupportable.

Last year, did he not vaunt, in London, about representing, all by himself, French Letters? The insolence was so great that the journals even, ever disposed however to suck the uppers of the conqueror's shoes, grew indignant for one or two minutes. Useless and mildly menacing barks that were unable to trouble him.

That did not stop him any less from promoting himself. Students, so literary, as everyone knows, attentive to the pari-mutuel machine and to the lever, need him to preside over their feasts. The Scandinavians congratulate him and the English even translate him. He is consulted on all matters, having become the Thinker, as old Hugo was before him, and his miter preponderates at divers councils. Finally the Academy, daughter of the ages, begins to redden with concupiscence for this osprey.

The need to write a book such as *Lourdes* imposed itself on his vigilant mind. For a period of time, in fact, restorative attempts on sepulchral Catholicism had manifested themselves. Inexplicable people, such as Paul Verlaine, unsettled the imagination of young men by speaking to them about the Holy Sacrament and Prayer in lines of unmatched length. A vain multitude who did not read exclusively *Pot-Bouille* or *Joie de Vivre* rushed out to join pilgrimages. The urgency exploded with the publication of a prophylactic book.

The apostle of the gentiles of Positivism did not hesitate. Equipped with a prayer book and I do not know what manuals of facile piety, in order to not come up completely short on theology and liturgy, neglecting perhaps a little too much of canonical law, he proceeded to document the "Idol" that is venerated in the Pyrenees where the mountain dwellers, one does not know why, abstained from beating him within an inch of his life with their canes, as several journals had joyously announced.[7]

It is a little much all the same that this bison, who has not even the excuse of acting like a writer, should be allowed to place his parcel of manure on a great thing that, for us, brings tears to our eyes!

"The miracle of Lourdes, a fairytale, so touching and so infantile!..." he says. "The Church, incapable of battling the *unleashed winds of superstition*, has resigned itself to giving its faithful this idolatrous cult that it felt they were eager for." Do you see the hypocrite?

And he speaks of Faith as a "beautiful flower of ignorance and naivety..." of "those souls of children who completely abandon themselves to the least caress of legend." What style, gentlemen!

That simpering, ingratiating, and unctuous tone that recalls in a big way the *sympathetic Matthew* and other sorceries by the late Renan, is a novelty for M. Zola, who was, until recently, such a beautiful brute. Evidently, he prepares his acceptance speech before the French Academy.

He is Impartiality itself, he knows everything, he understands everything and he makes himself everything for everybody. A heart of gold! "Let us not make anyone despair, let us tolerate Lourdes... *However*, believe me, it is cowardly and dangerous to let superstition live. From now on, would it not be better immediately to have the audacity to operate brutally on humanity, by closing the miraculous Grottos where it goes sobbing and give it the courage to live a

---

[7]Original footnote: See, among others, the *Authority*, July 26, 1892.

real life even in tears?"

Behold, we have gotten to the bottom of it. He has come to shut down the Grotto, – out of love. His reasoning tells him that it is preferable to read *Nana* than the Office of the Holy Virgin, that the two hundred thousand annual pilgrims would do better to buy his Rougons rubbish than to pile into the wagons, and, because the Immaculate makes miracles, the cretin will break everything, smash everything while turning himself into one.

V.

And he pulled it off quite well, my faith! his little miracle. Oh! it is a nice story.

It has to do with an "irregular person of hysteria," it goes without saying, as all the saints must be and all women who do not live exclusively for making love in the "the open air" from morning to night, according to M. Zola's physiology.

"Her hair covered her like a golden cloak." This novel image which reappears here and there, as do others by this author, is the *single* trait that he can offer to describe for us the young person, on whom he appears, moreover, to have exhausted his imagination and his brush. I believe, however, that she has an "apron of snow" and a "turtledove's coo," but I am not entirely sure of it. These objects of luxury perhaps appertain to someone else.

As for the good man that accompanies his dying girl to Lourdes, he has of course a "bird brain."

Once again, that is how how one *writes* when one is papa Macquart.

But the finest character, the protagonist of the book, is the girl's lover, a preacher naturally. My God! He has not slept with her, if you will. His soutane gets in the way a little. But it is not desire he is lacking.

The abbot Peter is one of those priests, *like so many others*, "a priest who lacks faith, who practices his profession *chastely*, honestly," as M. Zola does his own, without any doubt.

One has to believe that our poet considers this idea both strong and dazzling, for I read it – identically expressed – at least five times, on pages 34, 273, 274, 319 and 597.

It would be unfair to demand that a thinker as overworked as M. Zola is should find the time to question whether a man who is condemned to live a lie twenty-four hours a day, without mentioning the sacrilege, is precisely an honest man. Let us leave that alone.

Besides, one is a man or one is not a man. And this one here "is not a man, because he is a priest." Consoling truth that one finds *ne varietur* on nearly every twentieth page, from beginning to end.

Is it not obvious that "bravery, reason, life, real men, real women" is all about copulating energetically, until one falls over dead!

In the end, abbot Peter is a good priest who speaks well.

They arrive in Lourdes. Procession of sick people to the pool. Procession of the Holy Sacrament. Procession with flames. The amorous adventures of a man with a Hospitaller Sister of Salvation *locked up together for three days in a closet*. Pictures of crowds and accosted priests. Prayers, canticles, vociferations, garbage, and trinkets of every sort.

The young sick girl is suddenly healed, after abundant supplications. Do not forget that she was one second earlier about to give up the ghost.

The naïve crowd shouts that it is a miracle. But abbot Peter, who has almost as much genius as M. Zola, knows perfectly well what to believe.

A young doctor with an extraordinary intelligence had announced to him, before their departure, "with a calm and smiling attitude, how the miracle might be accomplished similar to how lightning strikes, at a moment of extreme emotion, under decisive circumstances that would succeed in relaxing the muscles. Transported with joy, the sick girl would rise and walk, legs immediately feeling light, relieved from the heaviness that made them feel, for such a long time, like lead, as if that heaviness had melted away, had flowed into the earth. But above all the weight that crushed the stomach, that climbed, that ravaged the breast, strangled the throat, would go away, at that moment, in a prodigious flight, *in a tempest blast*, carrying away all illness. Was it not like this that, in the Middle Ages, people possessed by spirits let escape through their mouth the devil that had so long tortured their *virgin* (!?) flesh?"

And there you have it, the sick girl is healed by "the power of decoupled auto-suggestion."

Science, as one can see, admirably explains these phenomena. When it cannot explain them, it leaves them be. But that does not prove anything, on the contrary.

M. Zola, having thus brought his prodigy to a good ending, sheds a last tear on the celibate "haughty," his abbot Peter; he abandons himself, once more, to some thoughts that are as *novel* as his prose; recognizes benevolently that he himself is reason, au-

gust Reason; comes to sit down for a few moments, to
dream, on his knees, like a great traveler; implores "a
new religion that might fill him with hope"; and pro-
nounces, while wrapping things up, that Bernadette,
the seer of Lourdes, had been "the terrible lesson, the
holocaust cut off from the world, the victim condemned to abandonment, solitude, and death, struck
with the degeneration of *not having been woman*, nor
spouse, nor mother, *because she had seen the Holy
Virgin*."

Cretin!

Part the Second

The Last Childhood

Extract from a Letter to a Soldier

April 25, 1899.

"*... You write to me that your position as an officer makes you, in my eyes, frivolous... But that is completely crazy, my friend! Am I an editor at* l'Aurore! *How could you not know, having read my material, that, with a Priest's reserve*, I always put the military above everything? *But you must understand...*

"*To put an end to that dirty Dreyfus affair, I am quite compelled, in spite of the extraordinary slander on the part of a large number of my friends, to consider it highly likely that the unfortunate man expiates on Devil's Island another person's or other people's crime, and that the superior command of our army is entrusted, for quite a long time now, to some really fine fellows. They are a laughing stock and a disgrace the world over.*

"*Dreyfus would have consequently been the victim of an awful in-*

iquity. Ah! well, and then? There are one million two people like him, each generation, and nobody talks about it. The interesting thing for me would be to know, actually, WHAT he is expiating over there, that prisoner. Because God is infinitely fair and each man, in this world as in the next, always *gets what he deserves.*

"That man there was rich. What was the source of his wealth and what did he do with it? Just as he pays for others, in the penal colony, who knows if someone does not pay for him, in an even more dreadful manner, at the back of some den. Along with that, what else needs to be considered?

"Outside the military, look at the legion of evildoers that rally around this affair, for or against, *from Hanotaux and Drumont, not to mention that imbecile Rochefort, as well as the filthy Cretin Émile Zola and all his clique.*

"But, once again, God knows what he is doing. You will see what kind of pit France falls into..."

– Léon Bloy

The Church sees souls.
Monsieur Émile sees monetary systems.

When certain events that were

nobody's concern forced me to quit France, last winter, for an indeterminate number of months or centuries, a friend, intent on pleasing me, favored me with a subscription to l'Aurore.

This respected rag seemed, in fact, suited, more than any other, to my edification.

Although living in a hole for Protestants of the Cimbrian Peninsula[8], I was able to enjoy, as well as in Paris, the ineffable prose of the new novel by Zola.

Incapable of adjourning my transports, I had the beneficial idea of relieving myself, each evening, after reading this rag.

The pages that follow – more or less copious extracts from a "Journal" that I will publish in the future – are the result of this practice.

– Kolding, this 9th day of October, 1899, Feast Day of Saint Denys.

* * * * * * * * * * * * * * * * * *

May 17. – Read in *l'Aurore* of the 15th, the first serialized installment of "Fecundity," a new work by the Cretin. It is over. The swine absolutely no longer writes.

May 18. – I would like, each day, after read-

---

[8]Cimbrian Peninsula: Jutland.

ing the serialized installment by the Cretin, to consign here, for the profit of the most distant posterity, several critical remarks or observations on this work. Unfortunately, Zola is the first man in the the world to say nothing in thousands of lines, precisely *nothing*. As regards judgments or opinions, his intellectual level is so low that the crappiest analysts do not dare descend there.... As for his literary form, it is at the same level as his heart, that is to say beneath every-thing.

I imagine that the funny man did not *give away* his paper, but that he made his very worthy friends pay for it dearly enough, and that these latter, when they are gathered together, must be scarcely put out to treat their heroic and venerated master as a "nag, scoundrel, bastard, horrible boor, etc." I believe I can hear from here the aristocratic voice of Vaughan, qualifying the great man as an "old cow."

One speaks currently of his "exile." We have gotten to the point now where an individual is glorified who scampers off at the hour of danger. *The Hegira of Zola*. What a chapter for the history of the end of the century!

May 19. – I was looking for a word to characterize Zola's stupidity. It is not only exorbitant. It is strange and dirty. It is a stupidity that would have served to rinse something.

But the more than probable cause of success, once again, is the pornographic slovenliness already caught glimpse of. Ah! he sure can dedicate himself to his career!

Only, in order to follow him, it is not enough to possess an unclean soul, one must also have a strong stomach. His naughtiness moreover stinks and would rather hasten one to virtue. It would appear that this is what his public needs.

May 20. – More of the excrement. Nothing to extract, even with red pincers. The impotence of the miserable man is something that ought to make bad Angels whisper. As for his baseness, I renounce trying to find a word to express it.

May 21. – Always at the same level, the serialized installment. I find myself rubbing elbows with concierges full of commonplaces and inexhaustible blathering, where the only things talked about would be sex and money, twenty-four hours a day. In fact, what other things could interest the Cretin?

Just read the sublime *Life* by Père Damien, missionary to the Lepers of Molokai, one of the Sandwich Islands, who died, in the end, of the horrible disease. *"We other lepers*," he said, – *before* being contaminated – to his frightening listeners, in the miserable church where the faithfuls' exhalations snuffed out the candles...

What an image, when one has just come away from reading Zola!

May 22. – "... Then, there had been the extraordinary story of her marriage with baron de Lowicz, her escape into the arms of that swindler, who had the beauty of an archangel." (!!!) It is the imbecilic female that all the Cretin's novels are peppered with for twenty years now. I would have been quite afflicted if I had not encountered that woman.

"Very rich," naturally; who laughs "with her white teeth of a *she-wolf*, between her bleeding lips"; who is "really adorable, with an irresistible desire";

what am I saying? "with the charm of a *magician* whose eyes burn, empoisoning hearts"; who "preserves her attitude as an invincible lover" and who places on her lovers' mouth "her small, long and enveloping hand." The man who writes that is the *prince of French prose writers.*

It must be that this prince was repulsed and loathed by the loosest of whores, so that by sixty years old, he should have, at this point, dry mouth at the mere thought of a skirt!

It is to be remarked that all the characters, without exception, that is to say many families, have agreed to talk about nothing but coitus and abortion during the three or four months[9] that *l'Aurore* will publish this filth, which is incontestably generous. But what to say about this society of boot wipes and wealthy fried potato merchants whom Zola treats like a very lofty aristocracy?

May 23. – *L'Aurore* came out the day before yesterday, on Pentecost Sunday. On this day of the Holy Spirit, what will the Cretin tell us? Nothing that has not already been said, a very large number of times, because this prince of prose writers has the speciality of giving only what is to be swallowed up again, indefinitely, and offering up for consumption three hundred lines of commonplaces everyday.

"Her gay round face, with black headbands, had the delicacy of a flower." That is an old portrait of a young woman, dusted off often enough! Also noted is a small devout woman "already on the road for every kind of folly, *still taking communion*, but confessing her sins, familiarizing herself everyday

---

[9]Original footnote: Five months. This publication lasted FIVE MONTHS!!!

with the idea of fault." Buck up, sow! Émile is watching out for you.

May 24. – Good page by the Cretin. "Look then in the New Testament for 'Be fruitful and multiply and fill the earth' from Genesis? Jesus has no fatherland; no property, no *profession* (!!!!!), no family, no wife, no child. *He is infecundity itself.*" Behold finally where he wanted to lead us. THE INFECUNDITY OF JESUS! Idiotic scum.

May 25. – The Cretin explains to us finally, finally! his personal infecundity. It began to get a bit *comical*, if I dare say so, the obstinateness of this gelded novelist shooting his mouth off against the contemporary infecundity of loins and uteruses.

Here we go: "You cannot deny, my dear sir, that the strongest, the most intelligent, of men are the least fecund. *As the brain of a man enlarges, his generative faculty weakens.*" In other words, Émile Zola has too much mind to make babies. This great and *fecund* idea was unveiled for me, previously, by Huysmans. That will be quite enough for one day, no? and all the rest would appear to fade into the background.

What good would it serve, for example, to note "the yellow danger," that is to say the Chinese invasion of Europe, not at all a banal idea, except that, as you can see, Émile believes it, however, undoubtedly, engendered by himself, wrung out, like wastewater to empoison congresses with, from the rinse-bidet sponge that is his – *broadened* mind?

May 26. – Overcoming a violent nausea, I take up my reading again. The mailman having brought me two issues at once, I have consumed them one after the after, at the risk of kicking the bucket.

The joy of subscribers must be great, because it is delightfully smutty, there is no way to deny it, and one can expect that it will become smuttier still. In this ultra comical novel, all the world seems to have their nose in everyone else's behind. There is not one character, male or female, who thinks of anything other than the friction more or less subtle, more or less refined, of fresh meat... Ah! the erotic outburst of the Cretin is spectacular!

But one is a thinker all the same, it must not be forgotten. For example: "Nations will disappear again. Others will replace them, and *how many thousand years* will it take to arrive at the last judgment, made of truth and peace, conquered at last?..." Behold how one gains the upper hand on Bossuet. Émile has already rendered us that service, in his great evacuation of the bowels on Rome. I do not have the text at hand any more, naturally. It has been quite a while since it disappeared down a hole, but I recall the globe was compared to a bobbin around which civilizations were wound and unwound successively and indefinitely... Until the West becomes completely senile, like the author, the East grows young again, and *vice versa, in æternum.*

For what there is of style, it is nonexistent, always the same stuff, the same indestructible and indefectible clichés, for thirty years now. When one has just finished reading a poet and then tries to read Zola, one feels as though he has fallen into the loo.

May 27. – Ah! but the Cretin's novel becomes completely stupefying. Will I be forced to abandon my quotidian note-taking? It is evidently too easy to predict how this idiotic and foul story will end. A matter, besides, that holds no interest. But there they are, twelve installments waiting for me, twelve times three hundred lines, filled exclusively with conversations by folk belonging to various classes of society and who have no other interest whatsoever except how to avoid making babies. Any other subject matter is excluded. There is talk only of fraud, of the desire to be satisfied without inconvenience, of individuals with gross carnal appetites, of women who are amusing, or not amusing, in bed, etc.

The curious thing is that this pig suffering from Priapism, while waiting for general paralysis, but who – with a senile obstinateness – wants nevertheless to be a *Moralist*, lacks the audacity of obscenity. At every moment, one senses that he is dying with the desire to articulate some filthiness, but he does not dare.

May 29. – Clémenceau, whose attacks on mediocrity seem to grow more frequent when he is in contact with the Cretin, and who willingly gives us "Saint-Bartholomew's Day Massacre, Revocation of the Edict of Nantes, White Terror, etc."; Clémenceau, I say, rises with *authority* against obedience, against the spirit of obedience that "degrades" man and which he believes is "servitude." The servitude to Gohier[10], one might be tempted to say. Not to Zola. The Cretin is much lower, and he would need the Prophet's[11] chariot of fire to rise as high as those idiocies.

Must it be that Clémenceau, who is not however a brute, like his colleague Urbain and some oth-

---

[10]Gohier: the reference is most likely to Urbain Gohier (see next paragraph), one of the writers at *l'Aurore*.

[11]Elijah, in the Old Testament.

ers, – and whom one could even call a writer – is consumed with ambition to put on that uniform of commonplaces, that vile tabard of subaltern Free Masons, recently lifted from a table d'hôte for salesmen or from behind a cobbler's workbench! It is, moreover, a strange sensation to think about the frightening tyrant who would at the drop of a hat become a domestic and willingly, to boot, if he unexpectedly became a master!

Reading the thirteenth installment by the Cretin, my mind turns immediately to Huysmans, and I wonder if he is not in some way connected with the spirited movement that brought "Fecundity" to fruition, and if Zola, in many a page, vomitive otherwise, God knows! had not had the intention of confounding an old disciple whose recent Catholicism must have made him feel indignant. Because the author of "Lourdes" is certainly incapable of doubting the *Catholicism* of the author of "The Cathedral." They are, to be sure, clairvoyant, the one as much as the other.

Come to think of it, I remember Huysmans expressed to me, – how many times! – his horror of children, going so far, with not the least compunction, as to formulate theories on abortion, vaunting even to have put them personally into practice. Now that he is a Catholic, – the Catholic of his three last plots – Joris-Karl, does he still think like this?[12]

---

[12]Original footnote: I am told that Huysmans has taken, not the *veil*, but the Benedictine habit, at Ligugé. I see no need to be in a hurry to congratulate the family of Saint Benedict. I worked, for four years more or less, to inseminate Christianity into this novelist come out of Médan. Ungrateful earth and rude labor!

Others reap the harvest. May they enjoy it! I do not envy them, and I will wait, to modify my feelings or my views, until it is

But the Cretin's case is something altogether different, and, without a doubt, I suppose quite gratuitously that he has his reasons. He himself has no need for theories, nor thoughts, nor even the least defined embryo of the most inferior concept. What would he come up with? He is *all tail*, if I dare risk this trope which, alone, renders my thought, and the frauds, the empty embraces, the sterile matings, the semen scattered randomly and which "hardens and dries," "*the slop pails* next to the washstand, full of a soiled, wasted life, that one dumps down the drain," all that torrent of rubbish, what else is it but the occasion, hoped for for twenty years, of a fairly mature senility that should allow the mandrill, set up as a transcendent moralist, to dare pull down his trousers finally and pollute himself before furnished lodgings.

May 30. – One thing I do not tire of admiring in the Cretin's installments is the impotence, the *infecundity* of the author. It is consternating and even a little diabolic to read this monstrous, infinite, chatter, that deluge of words, pages after pages of it, which never ends, in order to keep trotting out indefinitely a miserable commonplace, without any hope of encountering, I do not say an idea, but an image, the semblance of an image that hasn't been served up a million times already! It makes one think of a cadaver masturbating.

"... And he was still thinking of beds in the caserns where four hundred thousand young men sleep alone, unproductive, etc." Does this not sound like the lamentations of a brothel manager whose business is threatened? The respectable man would

proven to me that this "oblation" is anything more than a *literary gesture*. – Kolding, April 1900.

like to give females to all those males.

At this point, it is just a matter of semen, milt, fish roe, "eggs that *flow* (sic) in the veins of the world, etc." And such is, in five hundred lines, the exclusive meditation of the young father of a family who goes to ride a train, on the Northern railway, in order to lie down gently with his wife, but who, having gotten her period, would rather live it up instead, if M. Émile were good enough to allow her to do so.

One guesses how it will end. Here we find him back already walking along the boulevards, having decided to miss his train. It was to be expected. The Cretin's schemes are not complicated enigmas and one cannot say that he was gifted with an imagination full of surprises. Until tomorrow then, doubtless, and the days that follow, the spicy recitation of that night of love. With the svelte and rapid form that one is familiar with, there is reason to presume that this episode will not surpass three thousand lines.

May 31. – Deception and humiliation. The hero of *Fecundity* will not live it up, not that night at at least. M. Émile will not allow him.

He dashes onto the train and comes to find his wife who is waiting for him "under the stars, with her small and firm breasts, her cheeks like savorous fruit, and her skin with a milky whiteness that her admirable black hair accentuates even more..." Hey! damn!

June 1st. Continuation of idyllic coituses. How nice vice seems compared to the virtue offered by Émile Zola!

June 3. Yesterday and today's serial install-

ments. The continuation of virtue. The maker of children, three quarters of whom are seduced by the
Malthusian eloquence of M. Émile's clients, tries to
persuade his wife to stay there with him. She does not
seem to want to bite. Boredom that is nearly unsupportable. Impossible to get away, to withdraw, to be
alone in whatever way possible. Not even a stupidity
a little more shocking than others. I cannot help citing
however the little children asleep "like little Jesuses
and smiling like angels" or other treasures of that cal-
iber. One thing keeps coming back, over and over
again. It appears that he is proud of it. "To live well,
one must love life." To hell with the senile old man! I
truly believe that I have just undertaken a nasty job.

June 4. – Today our Cretin gets to the end of
the "first book," one hundred pages, at least, in which
he has spoken only of things related to sex; it is a
wonder, completely unique to Zola, of a stubborn, en-
raged, not-to-be discouraged reiteration, of the same
objects, by means of the same formulas, the same
cliched expressions, and all this by employing the
granitic vocabulary of a street vendor, an engineer of
rural thoroughfares, or the secretary to a police com-
missioner touched by literature. One cannot think of
another popular novelist who could count, as much as
he has, on the stupidity or idiocy of his readers. And
we are merely at the dawn of filthiness, as this is only
the first book.

For all that, before setting down his light quill
– for even a short period of time –, he felt the need to
promulgate, once again, that the "most intelligent are
the least fecund." One has already read (*May 25*) this
lofty maxim, with its immediate application. Today,
he adds, by way of corollary, that "children cannot

ever emerge in such large numbers except from the manure of poverty," – which recalls that other haughty sentence that the mind's superiority consists in making money, – which is all about making oneself agreeable to Monsieurs the Boors and being commended to their goodwill.[13]

Finally, made lighter by this testimony, he allows that one should produce one more child in the house of the "little Jesuses."

"And they had the arrogance, the *divine carelessness*. Ah! what delights!... That was their *act of faith in life*, a *canticle* to fecundity, generous, inexhaustible creatress of worlds."

Ah! yes, what delights! the "delicious drunkenness" of these phrases regularly served up every year, in the same fine order, since the liberation of the territory! But who said that Zola was a man without religion?

June 5. – (in the Octave of the Holy Sacrament). SANCTIFICATION OF SUNDAY. *Divine office.* "... A veneration seized him, he adored it (the good goddess of brilliant flesh, the gentleman's lady, of course), like a devotee in the presence of his God, on the threshold of mystery... *He uncovered her belly, with a religious gesture.* He contemplated it, it was so white, of so fine a silk... He bent over, he kissed it *reverently*, while investing all his tenderness in that kiss, all his faith, all his hope (one is no longer theo-

---

[13]Original footnote: Syllogism of the *perfect* democratic Boor. Major premise: The most intelligent people are the least fecund. Minor premise: But children can never emerge in large numbers except from the *manure* of poverty which is, by consequence, that of stupidity. Conclusion: therefore intellectual superiority consists in earning money by the rudimentary means of poor people's children. – Monsieur Émile.

logical). Then he stopped for a moment, like one of the faithful in prayer, placing his mouth lightly...” Nothing remains but to retire on one's tippy-toes, after having cast a last glance full of respect in the direction of the "slop pail."

The celebrated senile old man does not forget to tell us that this pious ceremony takes place on Sunday. It is in this way that he understands that the Day of the Lord should be sanctified. When great men who are decrepit, or not yet decrepit, undertake to replace God, this is what they will find.

June 7. – A familial Berquinade[14] of six hundred lines, for two days straight. Let's go! little children, come and give a nice little smile to your uncle M. Émile who loves you so much. Da, da, da, da, da, – Ga, ga, ga, ga, ga.

This illustrious and sympathetic personage is, moreover, on the point of returning to France, if, however, he ever left it – which is up for debate.

One article of four columns and thirty thousand characters to inform us that he desires to return *in silence*. Barely a few words about Dreyfus. He speaks principally, of course, about himself and the "tortures" of his exile.[15] They could have been attenuated, I imagine, by some softness. The sufferings in

---

[14]Berquinade: after Arnaud Berquin, author of stories for children.

[15]Original footnote: The *tortures of exile* of M. Zola who skedaddled, after having walked off with fifty thousand francs of his friends' money, I like to believe, because such is the just price of a serialized novel by this disinterested cretin! Behold the man who takes us furiously far from Devil's Island where one pleasantly amuses himself, as everyone knows!

Take off your mask then immediately, egoist and cowardly cockroach!

exile of a novelist who *earns* two or three hundred thousand francs a year with a single smutty book, do not seem to need to occasion a national mourning.

Did he not have, besides, the consolation of writing "Fecundity," and the more sublime consolation of knowing that he – he alone – "had one passion only in life, that of truth... that, for forty years, he had *served* his country by his quill and *sang* of France in over forty works already?..." Finally, could he not have borne himself such comforting witness "to having carried *the little sacred lamp,* which would shed light on the world if the powerful, evil men came to put out the sun!!!?, etc."

Would that he had not then spoken of recompense. The dear man had no just desert. "I want people to say of me that I was neither stupid nor nasty." That is all he asks for. As for those base and foolish souls who calumniate him, who hurl outrages at him, not just today, but since he began writing, he protects them with his "indulgence of a *poet*, fully satisfied with the triumph of the ideal."

Fundamentally, despite the "serenity of his soul," he is green with fear that he will be reproached for having made off in order to escape the gendarmes, and another, quite precise, but far more icy fear that he will get finally what his labors deserve. Who knows? the conscience of that scoundrel is not perhaps completely defunct.

June 8. – "Queen (a girl thirteen years old) began to laugh, *already knowledgeable* no doubt in the ways of the world, when Ambroise came to shout at her mother that she was his little woman and that Rose was their baby." It is so pure, so virginally symbolic, that *fleur de lys* in a chamber pot sitting on M.

Émile's work table!

It appears, besides, that this filth – or any other filth, naturally – is "higher and truer than the ado-
ration of the Virgin." What resource all the same,
what senility, and just like that a writer portrays
things!

June 9. – Conjugal ignominy called fraud and
which returns continually in this filthy book is
judged, this time, and qualified, as *culpable practice*.
Come on! Émile, it is too stupid, in the last analysis.
If there were no God, as you seem to claim endlessly,
like so many cobblers before you, where do you get
the culpability of whatever or whomever? How can
that be! Tomorrow I will be a pile of rot, nothing
more, and I would go without laughing, today, just
like that. *I would obey the catechism, without believing it*! What crap!

"... She spoke of Dr. Boutan, wishing that
someone *repeats* to him, etc." The cretin has defini-
tively dropped the imperfect subjunctive.

Hold on! Hold on! Here is our glorious repa-
triated author copping it at the publishing house itself.
The unprecedented presumptuousness of his article
from the day before yesterday has made Bernard
Lazare indignant, he who was, in reality, the first, and
only, person four years ago, to occupy himself with
the Dreyfus affair, who saw Zola standing up suddenly from between his legs, – *when the affair was ripe*,
ready to pick, – and who, after attaining the victory, is
not even mentioned once.

Bernard Lazare, a decent writer and without
speaking at all about "the holy little lamp," protests,
in quite strong terms, against this ignoble silence. He
does not name the funny man, but one can see quite

clearly that he is thinking about him, when he speaks, for example, of the workers "at the eleventh hour."

"I'm the one who did everything!" bellows Zola, "me the Apostle! me the Martyr! me the Citizen! *me*! me! ME!" It is about time that that pile of * be thrown into his face. I imagine that the decent fellows at Vaughan's place are equally upset.[16]

June 10. – Senile patter about wet nurses. One does not ask for ideas, oh! no, but a word, nothing but a very little word by a writer, which never comes. Literature by cattle merchants!

June 11. – All that I could gather: "As for Santerre (Paul Bourget), he was none other than the good friend he had wanted, one day, to enter into the room where his wife was taking a bath in order to show him just how *amusing* she looked in the water." That does not happen in any other way, one has to believe, in the places that Monsieur Émile frequents.

To a friend:
"... I hope, however, that some people will do me the justice, when Zola's surprising viciousness is brought to full light, when his friends or pretended admirers of the present are compelled to push him back down into the deep latrines whence he came, – which must certainly happen much sooner than anyone imagines.

"Already the miserable man has half-betrayed himself in the mon-

---

[16]Vaughan: Ernest Vaughan, founder (together with Georges Clemenceau and Urbain Gohier) of *l'Aurore* in 1887.

strously presumptuous letter entitled Justice, *wherein this threefold idiot, stuffed like a bird for thirty years now, speaks about the "tortures of his exile" – him! – and the bitterness that resulted when his literary life was "cut short." What a repugnant and hideous hypocrite. You will see what follows. Well, maybe, – but not without shame and horror – you will remember Léon Bloy whose warnings you scorned.*

"You are hypnotized to the point of writing to me that the Dreyfus affair is 'the greatest historic drama of the century'!!! on a par at least, by consequence, this movement of the bowels, with the Napoleonic Epic; with the Franco-Prussian War; with that torrent of black blood that is the highly mysterious and so little known story of Naundorff,[17] etc. You are delirious.

"You find the proof of a true 'grandeur' in J'accuse. *If that is the case, then I no longer understand at all why you read me and why you say that you admire me. You have no right. 'What difference does the imbe-cilic novel* Fecundity *make,' you add, 'next to so great a role, when one pos-sesses so powerful a lever? (!)' Yes, is-n't that right? what difference does it make that a so-called writer should*

---

[17]Naundorff: See *The Son of Louis XVI* by Léon Bloy, published by Sunny Lou Publishing.

*have polluted thousands of hearts, and
DE-GRADED the French language and
French spirit; what difference does it
make that at this moment even, – he
outrages God every day, in three hundred lines, – if he had shouted or ap-*
peared *to shout for Dreyfus? So be it,
but then what might you think of the
author of* Salut par les Juifs[18] *who sacrificed everything for things of so little
importance, other than that he is an
idiot or a lowly crafter of phrases?"*

– LÉON BLOY.

June 12. – Vaughan is the one who must not
be laughing! There must also be some pretty impreca-
tions being hurled about there, each night, in his editorial office, when he has to make room for this child-
ish installment whose frightening, homicidal boredom
becomes, day after day, more intolerable. Even turpitude becomes more rarefied. It becomes a very lowly,
monotonous gossip, which is perpetual and without
issue, in a world obsequiously abject where dreary
stupidity and comatose boorishness are balanced by
the *inexistence* of every character without exception.

Be on your guard! men of *l'Aurore*. You are
going to bore people!

June 13. – I really do not have the courage.
There is no way forward anymore. As regards recent
events, an important individual in this Danish town
speaks to me about Zola, and I am made to under-

---

[18] *Salut par les Juifs*: *Salvation Through the Jews,* idem.

stand, without surprise, that the last three novels (the *Three Cities*) were infinitely agreeable to Protestants who accepted, like articles of faith, the unsavory calumnies of this pompous manufacturer of mustard for the Riffraff. One knows that the most horrible filth acquires a divine taste for Protestants, when it has to do with swallowing them in opposition to Rome.

"– Zola's immense success is exclusively attributable to his filth." That, very spontaneously, in no way suggested by me, was spoken in the clearest manner possible by my interlocutor.

The present alliance between Jews and Protestants represented, in sum, by the Cretin, is, all the same, an unprecedented monstrosity. What is Protestantism, in effect, if not the fall of Christianity, the negation of the Essence and the Substance made manifest? When a man says: "I am a Protestant," it is as if he were saying, "*I do not exist.*"

The Jew, on the other hand, is the antagonist, in the Absolute sense of the word. He is the Older Brother who has separated from the Younger – because the fat Lamb was killed in the house – until the Spirit of God grabs hold of them, and reconciles them in Unity. The Jew and the Catholic are equal by their common extraction and ought not to ally themselves with Protestants any more than masters ought to marry their domestics.[19] A Jew can esteem a Catholic, without ceasing to hate him, and *vice versa*, but how in the world could either of them not scorn a Protestant!

---

[19]Original footnote: I was mistaken just now. When a man says: "I am a Protestant," it is as if he were saying: "I refuse to wash the dishes" or "I prefer to wash the dishes." That depends on his nature and principally on the circumstances.

June 14. – An admirer of the Bastard wrote to me:

"Fecundity! *Ah! We are so far from the* Iliad! ! ! *We are among the Bourgeois!... There is nothing to say, we are there for sure! It could not get any worse. And it is, really, I confess,* unbreathable, *and one is happy to have the consolation of reading several pages in the* The Woman Who Was Poor, Salvation Through the Jews, The Desperate Man, *and* The Ungrateful Beggar *to purify oneself.*

"*Beauchêne, Santerre (which appears to be Bourget), Séguin du Hordel (?) – oh! the puerility of that H! – and the wives!!! It is good however in that world there that we evolve, as much as one can* evolve. *What a bunch of rotten bastards!!!*

"*In all the novels by Zola that I have read, there have always been at least some murders, some dirty battles of self-interest, between the forward thrust of the bull and the bedding of cows combined with other bestial calvings. But, here, one gets out of a rape only by falling into difficult parturition or an abortion during an ovariotomy! The clinical stench in the bourgeois bed is barely interrupted for the rattling off of children that are made, have been made, and will be made or will not be made, or will be* unmade.

"We are at the point now where all the females in the book are already pregnant, from the last maid, concierge, patroness, fruit seller, and even visitors, whoever they might be, young or old! Which makes me presume that Zola himself will not be able to extricate himself, and I renounce, from now on, following along with him!

"All the same, when one can brave the abjection of the topic and the incontestable vulgarity of that style (?) or what substitutes for it, it is quite fine sometimes!"

June 15. – More nothingness, if one dare say so. A factory boss impregnates one of his workers and abandons her. Two girls fight in the middle of the workshop, as in "l'Assommoir." Then, there is the desolation of the parents of the girl who was seduced, who would like to settle their daughter's situation by money from the seducer, who refuses to go along with it...

Zola's language discovers the secret for being even lower than the things themselves!!!

June 16. – "... And he became superior, handsome and victorious, a man certain to win all the battles in life." It's one of fifteen or eighteen phrases written 3,745 times or thereabouts by the Cretin, for thirty years and going strong. He is keen on them. That much is certain.

The millionaire seducer is taxed five hundred

francs by Émile. O insatiable proxenete! Your cus-
tomers will leave you, my old Zola.

June 17. – The inside story of mid-wives. Occasion to deploy a little virtue. An attempt even at literature, the first I believe since the beginning. Poorly
recompensed, alas!

The unmarried mother with five hundred
francs, put up in a respectable home, declares to
"have never been to such a feast before, nourished
and taken care of, coddled from morning to night,
with nothing to do. 'You know,' she says, 'I ask for
one thing only, and that is that this lasts as long as
possible.'" The 32nd installment ends on this dazzling
note.

June 18. – Finally, behold incest this late in
the game; I did not dare ask for it.

Zola's indigence of imagination, even when it
comes to filth, is so surprising that his readers must
be yearning for the novels by Richebourg or Mon-
tépin, like cows in the desert for the pastures of
Canaan or Mesopotamia.

In *l'Aurore*:

> *"The telegram from Brussels*
> *announces that Antwerpen journalists*
> *are about to agree to offer Zola, by*
> *form of address, a copy of the letter*
> *"J'accuse," printed with the assis-*
> *tance of famous individuals from the*
> *publishing house of Christophe*
> *Plantin, which will give a particularly*
> *curious cachet to that homage.*

> *"The printing would have been*
> *performed by the art editor, M. Paul*
> *B., and the binding would have been*
> *entrusted to M. Jacques M.*
>
> *"The copy would moreover be*
> *signed by journalists who would have*
> *contributed monetarily to the confec-*
> *tion of this unique and marvelous*
> *copy."*

It is known that the Antwerpen, Parisian, London, Venetian, or Montalbanais journalists have not
got three cents to rub together, except when there is a
good piece of filth to cover. In this latter case, they
would be commissioned rather.

I have nothing to say to them by way of coun-
sel then, but too bad the bookbinder does not think to
consult with me for the choice of a *skin!*

June 19. – Today, a great attitude of bravura.
The Cretin brings out his woman #3, "brown hair,
thirty years old, tall, with fine traits, beautiful tender
eyes, *a charming and kind mouth.*" A single touch
and that is it. And it is in this way that the Master
paints a portrait.

This person pays a visit, of course, to the mid-
wife, where she has come to get rid of something
quickly, before the arrival, on a ship from India, of a
ravenous husband. An entirely original story. Still
talked about, it goes without saying, is the "superb act
of life," the "eternal stream of seed (he eats some of it
assuredly) that circulates in the veins of the world,"
because the style never stops being as unexpected, as
begrudged, as fresh, as virginal as the thought that it
contains.

June 20. – Enter the Abortionist. Fanfares.
Who was that old whore who said to me one day:
"Zola, he's my favorite novelist"?

June 21. – Appearance or vague desire for a
beginning of something. Émile seems to want to pun-
ish vice and reward virtue, – he cannot help it. But,
where is vice and, above all, where is virtue, in a
world imagined by this miserable Cretin. With him,
one never knows.

June 22. – One understands less and less. This
time, however, there is a woman killed by the Abortionist, easy enough to predict. The great writer, the
prince of prose writers, describes her to us as
"adorable, with a waxen pallor." Hey! hey! The same
prince sorrowfully remarks the absence of a wax *candle*!!!? near the rotting carcass.
There is a lot of talk of "crime" here. Poor old
man!
What if we stopped there, for a while, at least.
So little respectable as France has now become, since
it climbs into bed with imbeciles or pimps, I think
that it is, all the same, not permitted to scre...w it up
at this point. That would be too much. Silence then
and patience, for one or two weeks.

* * *

June 24. – "He had felt that Paris was *poorly
sown*." Oh! Octave Uzanne!

June 25. – "When one is a good honest
father...." – "He left him, *crushed and calm*." I believe you.

A friend writes to me: "The disgust that I have for Zola has grown precisely as a result of his being the author of 'J'accuse.' He must have, behind his act, a private motive whose ignominy is known by God alone."

June 26. – "... The naked belly, the sacred belly that *opens*, like the earth, under the germ, to give life... The creative desire of the world." I had promised myself however that I would keep quiet, but how can I resist that?

To a friend:

"... Someone told you that Zola cannot be reproached for earning three or four hundred thousand francs per year, by his books. Bourgeois opinion, filthy opinion.

"There is, in London, million-aire monopolizers who grow rich, from time to time, by several tens of millions of pounds, by unleashing packs of famished dogs on such and such a province in India.

"There are other speculators, English or American, who poison people by opium.

"There are also countless entrepreneurs spread out across the globe, who earn a lot of money from the traffic of human flesh.

"Etc., etc., etc.

"Your someone, who seems to have abandoned God for some time,

for only a short time now, is still capable, I hope, of thinking that all these monsters force-fed on gold deserved instead to be force-fed on excrement or to die by the vilest of punishments; but he does not at all think *it is okay to blame an individual who poisons* ONLY *men's souls, and who vilifies* ONLY *their intelligences, who outrages* ONLY *God, and who* gets rich *by this profession. One is always a good enough man, however, when one* has appeared *to dribble over Dreyfus, while sticking it to the imbeciles. O Tribulat Bonhomet[20]!"*

– Léon Bloy.

"P.S. In my capacity as an artist, I am for the Esterhazy villain against the Urban Gohier[21] villain.

"Ah! yes, certainly!"

June 27. – "Ah! the little devil, he eats me, he comes to reopen my *crevice*!" Émile!

June 29. – Remarkable article by the excellent, enfranchised Lucien Descaves[22]. Unexpected phrase depicting Mrs. Dreyfus whom nobody assists "carrying the cross," and who is "reduced to laying it

---

[20]Tribulat Bonhomet: the eponymous character of a work by Villiers.

[21]Gohier: one of the journalists at *l'Aurore.*

down in the street, *on a bench*, and lying down *next to it*." Hang yourself, Émile, hoist yourself up wherever you wish, behind the door of the latrine, for example. You will never find anything so fine.

Let us call out, in passing, that at *l'Aurore*, it is normal to hear such words as "cross," "calvary," and "drinking from the chalice," etc.

The Capuchins of lofty piety, such as Clémenceau, Gohier alias Brother Urbain, or that Lucien with the face of a baleful cobbler, are emotionally attached to those vocables, not at all borrowed from the Church, as one can see. Everyone knows that these dignified individuals would have something to say, all the same they should not pry open, each morning, the drawers of their old Mother who gave them her milk and whom they decry magnanimously, as would seem proper for free men.

Was I wrong, just now, to exalt Descaves so highly? Here is what I discover in my current installment. It has to do with a mother who is giving her breast to a boy. "And she did that in the sun which *bathed her in a golden light*, before the vast company of men who *watched her*, without shame or concern even for her being *naked*, BECAUSE the earth was *naked*, the plants and the trees were *naked*, flowing with sap." !!!!! That has got to hurt, Lucien.

Ultimately, why would I not dare to put forward a symbolic or allegoric representation of our Cretin's actual feelings?

Émile, completely naked, under a tree, and his face furrowed by those countless and celebrated *wrinkles* of Stupidity, so scrupulously depicted by

---

[22]Lucien Descaves: one of the editors of *l'Aurore* at the time of the Dreyfus affair, and author of *Héloïse Pajadou's Calvary*, published by Sunny Lou Publishing.

Henry de Groux; Émile playing the flute, watching the sap of men and women flow, – in the Forest of Bondy!

July 2. – Let us see what our author appears to have come up with:

A family, the type that represents Fecundity, becomes too numerous to be nourished, the father having only a modest employment. He makes up his mind, then, to fecundate the earth, at the same time that he continues to fecundate his wife. Encouraged by the Cretin who will laden him with every gift, who will mine for him with both hands the treasures of "modern science" – whose key he possesses quite happily – he goes on to become necessarily, and suddenly, a land-clearer of great genius, a thaumaturge of agriculture, who will make "milk and honey" flow, with biblical abundance, in the middle of the desert.

I am preparing then to reread several pages and several chapters pinched from the *The Country Doctor* or from *The Village Curate* by the great Balzac, and adapted by Zola!!!

July 8. – Where am I, after one week? I was sleeping so soundly! Having swallowed half a dozen installments, arid like valleys on the moon, where there is talk exclusively of wet nurses who kill[23], I just discovered, in the horrible purée, this: "The virgin is nothing but emptiness, the mother is the *eternity* of life" and "when we learn how to adore the mother, the fatherland will be saved...." *Let's go, children!* etc. Yes, without a doubt! ah! yes, I believe you. How

---

[23]Original footnote: Let's go! Émile, come back down to earth. Why wouldn't they kill, these women, *if that brings home the bacon*, given there is no good God?

is that now? o François Coppée! You are quite something, you: you know what it means to be a *mother*; you know what the *fatherland* is; you know, no less than Zola, what it means to make babies; and you know, above all, what it means *to write*! Come to terms with him then for this phrase that I dare qualify as *mystical*: "They found on a bench, near the tree, a big girl who was wiping her child's buttocks with a piece of journal." What journal? Who will tell us? o Coppée! What mysteries! and how impenetrable are the Ways! Everything ends by wiping the buttocks. Think about it!

After this discovery, I give up. Oh! this novelist who paints boors exclusively, in front of a mirror!

July 10. – Continuation of the wet nurses who kill. Fortunately, here is a letter from an excellent idiot to the journal, the *Friend of the Beasts!* It is entitled: "The Death of the Dog." In the "tortures of his exile," this Martyr, having barely thirty thousand francs by which to eat each month, sees himself deprived of a dog even, of a little dog that "for nine years, had never quit his side." And this little dog, which he had forgotten to kiss one last time, upset by his master's absence, died "just like that."

This is what it is like to be the Prince of prose writers! Behold for the ten-thousandth time this "just like that" served up for all nations of the world, since the Franco-Prussian War!

July 14. – It is exactly as I had predicted. Here we have, arrived in the mail, our "choice morsels" from *The Country Doctor* or from *The Village Curate*. It is probable that the second will be utilized most of all, as it has to do with "fecundating" a desert.

Everything will happen, clearly, without Balzac's admirable priest, without his sublime penitence, without the saved and *converted* multitude of indigents and bandits; but, on the contrary, in a display and a crescendo of cretinous boorishness, which the magnanimous poet of *Séraphita* never had the faintest idea of.

There are few things so completely sinister as the attempted effort, sometimes, by this Émile to demonstrate that he knows no less how to play the lyre than how to use the chamber-pot brush.

Thus, in the 12th installment, there is a mind-boggling parallel between the "little flowing of maternal milk" that flows "with a light murmur from its source" (!) and the noise from another fountain, useless until then, dissipated in the marshes, but "captured" finally by the genius of this Balzacian agronomist, with the virtuosity of fecundity, and which "descends along the rivulets towards burning lands."

No, one has read nothing, and will never read anything, if one has not read that.

July 16. – "One only makes babies by making love"! That there is the thinker's hammer. When Zola is not speaking precisely about sex, that is what he comes up with.

July 18. – "... That river of milk that had flowed from her... the good goddess, in constant fertility... the divine desire, the burning soul that the fields palpitate with."

We are at the 63rd installment. There are another good 40 or 50 to go, this bovine maternity, this idiotic pullulation! The Divine Image, such as the poor old Cretin's brain can conceive of it, smacks quite a bit of those idols of bygone theogonies that were represented by a double row of teats, like sows with a human face. He must think this *ideal* extremely new. He seems even to have gotten quite carried away with this discovery.

July 19. – "All the same," interrupted Bénard, his mouth full, "they could have, on the Sunday I spent one hour with you, informed me that they were going to *take everything away from you*. It is something, it seems to me, that a husband should know about, and that ought not to be done without his authorization... You yourself, you were not warned, you were totally stunned when you learned that you *no longer had anything*."

July 26. – It is high *melodrama* now and I have lost all my courage. Having arrived at the end of his roll of imagination (ah! it is not long), here is the unfortunate Cretin, not knowing what in the world to say anymore, *starting over again*. What would Père Ubu say about it, and Mère Ubu, without question the most decisive characters at the end of the century? What *word* would come immediately to their generous minds?...

I stumble across another story of ovariotomy, of a failed operation at the back of a *dive* (!) by an ungainly surgeon, – a stupid and vile story that can be read, every week, in every journal, written, with less words and more force, by any reporter you might run into at the station. But, today, the adventure is supererogatorily rehashed from an earlier chapter in the same book. The girl about to die on the same settee as her mother and sullying the same clichés with her filth. It is too much.

July 27. – Continuation of the story from yesterday, as imbecilic as it is filthy. "The adorable head of the child, *with waxen pallor... without a candle*"! (See above, June 22). One does not die, in works of the Princes of Prose!

In fact, how could anyone imagine I would not love these *adorable* women who regularly get their asses pounded by the Princes of Science, after they get off "work" at Zola's workplace, and who never forget to show up afterwards *on a filthy mattress* with a "waxen pallor and without a candle"?

Would this happen to be some great trick? To repeat the same thing over and over, to serve up obstinately and furiously again and again the very same recipes, the same phrases, the same verbs, the same adverbs, the same adjectives, the same pronouns, the same participles, and the same nouns, in view of obtaining the same hackneyed images, knowing that one is addressing the same intellectual public, – oh! how many times! – the pubic of Vaughans, Clémenceaus, Esterhazys, Urbain Gohiers, Merciers, Quillards, Couards, Gonses and Préssenses!!!... Émile! Come, let me kiss you!

July 31. – Nothing. Today's installment is nothing but a prolongation of yesterday's. Vomitive prelude to the great cantata, as loudly announced as protesting, about the unfortunateness of people devoted to God. We are about to see some pretty things! And *documented* above all, ah!

While we are waiting, here is an interview given by the Cretin. Somebody from *l'Aurore* rides to Médan on a bicycle. Sublime conversation with the patron who has not lost, nor risked – as some suckers claim – neither the fortune amassed by his tongue in the emunctories of the bourgeois, nor his reputation as a Bastard. On the contrary, of course!

The said interview informs us, first of all, this: "Cycling and photography, these are Zola's principal occupations while on vacation." This revelation holds nothing unexpected. He must necessarily collect stamps, take piano lessons, etc. this incomparable bourgeois is familiar with every bourgeois idiocy. One will learn, one day, that he introduces "thermometers into rectums," like Flaubert's heroes.

One also touches on, of course, the Affair. At which point, the interview becomes very interesting. "I was offered enormous sums of money to give conferences in America." He was offered treasures to write a drama or a novel on the said affair. "I refused them all"!

Here is a strategic position: "Exploitation, by me, of the Affair would be base and villainous." Doubtless, when the fruit no longer gives juice, one throws the zest into the garbage pale. However... villainous, yes, but why *base*? From the vantage point of the spectator, it seems to me that his turds even must shine at the center of constellations.

Some words on the *exile* – it was to be expected – and on a photographic "little twin" sitting on his bicycle, serving to hand out, in London, marvelous clichés. Finally, THE ALBUM OF EXILE!!! o Ernest! o Urbain! o Georges! o Francis!.... o my dear Cambronne!

Ah! I was almost going to forget this: "Since *Fecundity*, which *l'Aurore* published, I have written nothing SERIOUS!!!!!"

August 1. – Here we go: A teacher makes a

large hole in a door, to *see*. She leads a little girl to this hole and the innocent sees (how improbable!) Paul Bourget in the process of *fecundating* mommy. Below this, the innocent little girl asks that she be taken to the convent, immediately. The secret of religious vocations finally unveiled!

August 2. – Yes, Camille Lemonnier, you who, without being the legislator of any wandering people, have all the same written a *Genesis*, yes, Camille, it is a prearranged affair. With each installment, Matthew's female, – "good laying hen, good breeder," says the doctor – gives birth to one or more little ones. "Still possessing wealth and power," cries our imbecile, "a new force is *launched across the* WORLD...." Then, the attempt at raising on a grand scale. "It was the invincible conquest of life, *fecundity* ENLARGING throughout the galaxy; the work infusing, with each passing hour, more energy and more joy *in the veins of the* WORLD."

If this horrible macaroni has not been served up thirty times already, I beg someone to tear the skin off my back in front of a crowd.

The *world*! the veins of the *world*! "The regulating and CREATIVE work of the *world*." For nothing at all, he would write *savior* of the world.

These annoying stupidities are evidently easier to find than a thought or a beautiful image. It is an excuse.

August 4. – Heavens! What do I read? People who have not been seen, for many years, crying out: "What a lot of things! *That hardly makes us younger*." The Prince of prose writers plagiarizing Alphonse Allais!

August 5. – This time, there is a whore who decides, I do not know why, to breast-feed her infant, after having abandoned or massacred plenty of others. And, at that time, *she feels like a mother*!... This passage will be highly appreciated in the bordellos where ladies' sentimentality is at the breaking point, as everyone knows.

Ah! this is not the style that will pose an obstacle to enthusiasms! Never had the swine practiced so obscure, so dense, so compact, so inscrutable a gibberish. If Captain Dreyfus was a man, instead of an *innocent Jew* – which is quite certainly the last imaginable position one could take – he would send to the Chambers, to the ministers, to the potentates of this world, a petition to be reintegrated, immediately, with his penal colony.

August 7. – "Desire *burst into flame, divine desire* fecundated them... the necessary work, *fabricator and regulator of the world*... Still a child, still possessing wealth and power, a new force *launched across the world*... etc."

I ask this, calmly, of the twelve and a half very poor devils detached from the innumerable herd of boors, who hold deep in their hearts the traditions of some art, the loving memory of the antique nobility of French minds; I ask these wretched people what could be the formula of scorn applicable to a so-called writer who has the impudence to offer, in a so-called book like this, the same inane and low phrases as many as *thirty* or *forty* times, WITHOUT CHANGING A THING – and also what one should think of a public so debased as to admire a similar prostitution!

Of course, I have little love for Flaubert, and I

have already said why. But imagine this artist's howlings, he whose literary PROBITY was a quasi sublime thing and who grew exceptionally pale at the thought of repeating an adverb in fifty pages; what would be the indignation of the proud Normand *worker*, if he were still alive to stand witness to this base language!

Yes, I ask this with tranquillity, with humility, with the painful resignation of a hopeless supplicant... Silence!

August 10. – The filthy installment, interrupted for two days by the first hearing of the Dreyfus trial in Rennes, continues.

Of course Zola's impudence and stupidity have, by now, little chance of surprising me, but, it must be admitted, I receive a shock, a *little* shock, as Barrès would say, on re-reading, in continuation, the phrase that I had cited in the last installment. The same, the identical, the sempiternal phrase, indefatigably served up to the admirers of Urbain Gohier and Pressensé, for nearly two months now, that is to say with each birth in the house of Matthew, the fecund man who does not stop one minute – if only to read Zola! – to engender, to fertilize, to harvest, to gather, to acquire terrains, to practice virtue, to "harness the sources" and to disseminate the commonplaces.

"Still possessing wealth and power, etc." From one installment to the other, that is a bit steep, do you not think, Ernest? and fifty thousand francs for this ipecacuanha, it is handsomely paid all the same, o Vaughan! if I dare make use of that adverb from the Danube.

Even in Denmark, even in Jutland, one would be curious to learn the kind of reception reserved, in

France, for a less illustrious writer, were he of genius, who would undertake to mock his readers in this way.

August 12. – Enough to make one cry! Come on, Émile, why will you not stop? You are paid – much more than a thousand times what you are worth – Vaughan knows it only too well. Take your money and disappear. Once and for all, set your admirers free! Here we have two installments – six hundred lines nearly – to recount the death of a petty bourgeois, the miscarriage of two petty bourgeois, recognized by you yourself as an abortion. By you yourself!...

I have just read it without pleasure, but with attention. It is certain that you have made, this time, every effort imaginable to be *literary*, pathetic, irresistible. So that all the liquids that can be secreted by compassion flow at one time, you have fictively engendered by yourself an offspring, a stillborn Emiloide, "very calm, very white, his eyes closed, *as if he were sleeping.* In no way different, only thinner *in the stroke of lightning* (ah! yes) that had taken him away."

Is there any need to add that this sympathetic cadaver is, by you, surrounded by candles (finally!) and that he holds a crucifix in his joined hands? Is that not the ideal décor of all the bourgeois who come infallibly to weep at the first communion of their children – raised, otherwise, in the most complete infamy, while exiting the loge of the *Disciples of Memphis* or the *Clement Amitié Cosmopolite*[24], where they voted, before empty bottles, for the abolition of Christianity?

Their relatives, whose ignominy and stupidity

[24]Clémente Amitié Cosmpolite: a French Masonic lodge.

will not be discoverable until the Day of Judgment, those relatives admired by you, in spite of your *twenty-francs-per-line* protestations, "have aged ten years, *under that blow of the bludgeon*." As for visitors, friends of the family, they are encountered often in the modest cafes neighboring urban or suburban cemeteries that I believe it is pointless to mention.

Naturally, his fecund man is there, with his female who declares peremptorily that she has had enough, finally, of making babies and that "it is about time for her boys and girls to make babies."

August 13. – I did not dare believe it, but I am forced to surrender.

The unfortunate Cretin had the following idea:

"Some individuals, so-called literary, dare to suppose that I am finished. I will prove to them that I am just beginning. I will show myself *in a stroke of lightning*. Subito, without having warned anyone, I invent *the novel by refrains*, the novel of the desert that one will shout out at wedding parties. Ah! ah! my little detractors, you would not have foreseen this thrust!"[25] And he does as he says.

I cite this because it is the only way one will believe it: "Desire burst into flame, the divine desire fecundated them... the necessary, fabricating, and regulating work of the world... Still a child, still possessing wealth and power, a new force is launched across the world..." Yes, my poor old man.

It is disarming, no?[26]

---

[25]thrust: a fencing term.

[26]Original footnote: The unfortunate people who read this volume will see that a bit of deference for the public and, above all, my personnel disgust, have prevented me, at this time as at others, from citing the refrain altogether. (cont'd)

At this remarkable place, at end of the fourth book, – how many to come, o Lord? – everyone calves at the same time, at the fecund man's place, where "the bellies flow with an eternal fecundity."

Poor, great Balzac! so noble and so plagiarized by this tiresome hooligan whom he would not have hired to scrub the floor of his apartment – no, decidedly, I do not see it, reading such phrases, that make them swoon, without a doubt, all of Scandinavia!

"The grandmothers are pregnant, the daughters-in-law give milk already." Everyone works courageously to make babies. One would think he is at the stud farm or the breeder's. Zola mills about in that like a tadpole in his marsh.

August 18. – What intuition he had, refusing to go to Rennes! This Émile, decidedly, has an admirable instinct, I dare say infallible even, for *high tailing it*, when there is any danger afoot.

As for the installment, with no interruption, not for one second, from being fetid, it continues to be so annoying and so stupid that I do not imagine any other reader besides myself reading this filth.

What I do imagine quite well, for example, I believe I have already said it, and that is the editorial staff's rant when it must make room, each day, for a such a pain in the...

But doesn't one think it would be better altogether to be a dirty writer? Zola repeating to satiety the same imbecilic phrases, by impotence of imagination or penury of thought, could, with extreme rigor, be touching. But the sad turkey convincing himself that it is there that *art* lies, and putting those poor little devils of a phrase on his rump, and showing his tail feathers thereat, ah! really, you don't say.

However, I found this:

Two women on a settee, raise their skirts, successively: one to demonstrate that she has become too
disgusting to live it up, explaining, besides, with cries
of rage, that the ovariotomy made her incapable of
enjoying herself; the other to show "the occlusion of
her tubes"!!! which prevent her from having babies.
Antithesis of the "prude" and the "impure," in the
mind of the Cretin, who evidently puts great stock in
this display.

The fecund man, witness to it all, "stands
shivering."

Finally! we have some literature then to put
into the hands of the young people whom Mrs. Paule
Mink protects. It was about time.

August 20. – I tried to read in their entirety the
debates of the court-martial at Rennes. I could not do
it. It would need an act of God to finish that horrible
affair where everyone is abominable. The *innocence*
even of Dreyfus, while supposing it a foregone conclusion from start to finish, is almost uninteresting. I
see it very low, its face in the shadows and its feet in
excrement. Innocence proclaimed by Zola! It makes
one shudder.

The sempiternal installment of this funny man
continues. The senile repetition, instead of finishing
in its drivel, gives all indications of augmenting, men-
aces to devour everything in its path, like an alluvial
deposit of droppings.

Forced to rot away in Denmark, in the midst
of imbecilic Lutherans, what better journal than
l'Aurore to show me all the phases of degradation and
opprobrium undergone by France, which no longer
has the strength to get rid of its vermin! If I had a

friend devoted enough to purchase a subscription for me, in addition, to the "Libre Parole" or the "Cross", I would be set. I would have both extremities of the cow gut with which to strangle the noblest people that ever existed.

What is this Affair, however, that is spoken of around the world, if not an illusion, *the human and awful appearance of a DIVINE TRIAL that the time to shine some light on has not yet come?*

"... Santerre had decided to marry an old, extremely rich lady, logical end to this wily exploiter of women, *the lowest and greediest soul,* behind his posture of literate pessimist making money from the stupidity of a society in decomposition."

What does Paul Bourget think of these handful of lines, really quite good, which I was happy and stupefied to discover in the interminable pile of manure?

Would he not say that the old Cretin was gazing at himself, with narcissistic attention, in the very faithful reflection of a young psychologist's eyes?

August 25. – *The strength in numbers.* He has finally gotten to the point, the funny old man, the old sot, the old Cretin, I no longer say from the Pyrenees, but from whatever mountains he might have come from.

The strength in numbers! which the triple idiot calls in his patois "the victory of life," in an absolute incomprehension of all philosophical laws and of the very meaning of words, in the irremediable obstruction of what could have been his faculty to conceive, in his invincible ignorance of that infantine axiom that the strength of numbers is precisely, historically, physically, metaphysically and indisputably, *the tri-*

umph of death!

But let us examine this. When someone is strong in numbers, he is one hundred against one, ten thousand against one, one hundred thousand, one million against one, and there you have the very thing that pleases our lout. Therein lies his glory! that is what makes him rich and resplendent, and that is also, I dare hope, what will procure for him his forthcoming and incomparably ignominious burial in the most public grave in all the occident.

August 27. – The entire family of the fecund man on bicycles. "It is more modern... One does not hold his success against him. People who amass great wealth always finish by being right... The *conquering* family... The good fight of great culture...."

Then, all of a sudden, imitation, a thousand times unexpected, of the divine countess of Ségur. Poor Émile, unable, in his brothels, to acquire (conquer rather, that is one of his words) any facility in the language of the supposedly proper bourgeois, convinces himself finally to consult that respectable lady, so celebrated under the Second Empire.

And then, victory, o Henri Lavedan! there is a young virgin like those you sang about, an undismountable bicyclist and verified reader of your chocolate books, who talks about the "glorious consecration" of papa's property; who wishes that one go and find at the train station one does not know what future spouses, in view of a "repetition" of their imminent wedding; who says: "the royal couple... Our majesties... Their Majesties... the *prerogatives*... the queen-mother (that is to say, mama), the king and the princes," for quite a few pages. O you, Lavedan, nicknamed *mouthwash*, who taught the protocol of archduchesses, everything from how to use the thread and thimble to how to cut butter, why do you not kiss, on the lips, the great Cretin who gathers you up in his virtue and uses you?

August 28. – Continuation of the countess of Ségur and Henri Lavedan. It never ends these "princes, princesses, demoiselles of ceremony, pages, royal couple, Cinderella, prince charming, etc." Coupeau and Mes Bottes in red heels![27] There is an infanta who counts the procession and says: "That makes twenty... You are f*... (pardon!), you will be honored with such families! *The rabbits who see us pass are struck dumb with stupor and humiliation.*"

Émile is overjoyed to have finally *lifted* the language of old aristocrats.

August 29. – Today, the young girl with "rabbits" dies suddenly on her bicycle. I knew quite well that that would not work out for her. It is explained by our Cretin that what killed her, fundamentally, was the "imbecilic *love at first sight*" the which is "a *false* blindness that, with one stroke, *cuts down* everything in springtime." At which time the pious novelist lights economically "four candles" and lets out a cry: "Great *God*!"

One would love it, once and for all, to be sure, if they left them to Lucien Descaves, Clémenceau, Urbain Gohier, and some other ecclesiastics, – these tyrannical, inquisitorial, and outdated forms or vocables that make the adolescent and spiritual Paule Mink so justifiably indignant.

---

[27]Coupeau and Mes Bottes: two characters in Zola's *l'Assommoir.*

August 31. – Have I already mentioned the customary stupidity of Clémenceau, calling Dreyfus a heretic *because* he is Jewish? Clémenceau who appears to know the French language and even, it is said, a little bit of Greek, the savant Clémenceau believes that a Jew is a HERETIC!!! O Carthaginian hatred of the meaning of words! o Émile Zola! o Ubu! It is pointless to add that the said Clémenceau thinks he can destroy his unfortunate Israelite by hanging around his neck that bell of an old Vaudois cow that is three-quarters dead and stinking already on the mountain sides.

One knows that the Latin word *cum* is, of all prefixes, the one that determines, modifies, or particularizes the greatest number of French words.

September 1. – "Each time that abstraction has become the guide for humanity, civilization has deviated, lowered itself, contemned *life* in order to exalt a celestial glimmer, to *adore a star*, an idea, a nothingness." Alas! It is no longer Zola! as one might have thought. It is a writer, you understand what I am saying, a writer *knowing how to write*, a humanist full of philosophies and stories, that the single name of Zola made, not so long ago, grow pale with disgust. It is Remy de Gourmont having become inconceivably, unimaginably, the disciple of this master!!!!! (*Mercure de France*, September, page 769).[28]

A little further on, o Jesus in agony! the miserable man talks about Pascal and his "painful objections that *reason has to faith* in that obstinate and magnificent head of his."

Reason *opposed* to faith! Evidently that pleas-

---

[28]Original footnote: Jesus, in the past, healed the *lepers* by the dozens, by telling them to go "show themselves to the priests."

es Émile, warms admirably his brain. But the glorious shades of educators of the human spirit, from Aristotle to St. Thomas, what do they make of this imbecile having succeeded at finishing off a logician, a subtle poet, an ironist who was considered profound? It is enough to make one sob.

September 2. – Here we are at the 105th installment of "Fecundity." That is three and a half months already. One would think that it would have finished by now, arch-finished. The fecund man has engendered many children and he has become very rich, naturally, which ought not to surprise anyone. As for infecund folk, they rot away in abjection and ruin. Everyone knows that that is the law. As for the author, he has pocketed his 50,000 francs from Vaughan, while expecting another 250 or 300,000 more that divers other cashiers will offer him who are accustomed to taking a leak on Chatterton's tomb.

In brief, virtue is rewarded and vice punished, as always happens in this world. One would think it is finally time to write the word "*the end*" and to make way for a new sort of rubbish. Ah! well, no, no, and no! The Cretin does not disarm, the Cretin *recommences*. After having procreated a multitude of children, he has now devised to kill them off one by one, with each installment, in the same way as, previously, he bore them. Prodigious fun! There is, in the last two installments – more suited for toilet paper than reading material, – a rigged house designed to precipitate visitors into the depths, such as can still be found in some of the good old plays put on at the *Ambigu*[29] that Émile delighted in in his childhood. We find our-

---

[29]Ambigu: short for the Théâtre de l'Ambigu-Comique, a comedy hall founded in 1769 in Paris.

selves then ready to receive the 200th installment. Vaughan will get his money's worth.

September 4. – The "maternal devotion... the vengeful destiny that wanted this sacrilege... the ODOR OF NOTHINGNESS? (*vulgo*, phenol)!..." This entire episode of the imbecilic death of the fecund man's countless children, idiotically assassinated by the envious hatred of an infecund and stupid neighbor – this entire base scene of popular melodrama is enough to frighten, or inspire pity, according to one's temperament; to think that the author wanted to break, burn, steal, dominate everything under the sun, in order to show his worth finally before the statuary on Mt. Athos!

While we are here, at a vertiginous height, it would be appropriate to draw attention to the modern-day Atreides' fight to the death simply to know "who will own the factory." The purchase order, the sacred Purchase Order, such is the buskin worn by the Euripides or Sophocles of contemporary retail sales!

In one place, with the most pathetic tremolo, the fecund man, very disquieted, wishing to spare his female a dangerous emotion, she who was pregnant for the seventy-seventh time, in two hundred fifteen years, cries out with this: "No! I beg you, *God will descend*." I confess, I was stunned. But how briefly! On a second reading, I found this: "Denis will descend," – with some toilet paper, doubtless. Oh! sh**!

September 6. – "... she was at one and the same time the charm, the wisdom, the goodness, the single entire solid good fortune of the family. And he also was very good, very wise, too wise, they said, and she knew it and set out *en route*, on his arm, happy, certain that they would go together, at the same tranquil pace, until the end of their days, *under that limpid and divine sun of reason, in love.*"

After a very moderate calculation, each of these lines puts 15 francs, at the very least, in our imbecile's pocket. There has to be a hundred francs there. When the pig had written, between his coffee and his after-dinner drink, one hundred lines in this tenor, he had earned 1,500 francs, that is the ANNUAL salary of a poor employee of the railroad (exploitation service), who risks his life everyday. It is useful to note that the dirty cockroach is second to none when it comes to bellowing the word *Justice*!

From today on, reading *l'Aurore*, I see no means of believing in Dreyfus' acquittal. Had there ever been anything more manifest than the definite, absolute will, in anticipation of these debates, to condemn that Israelite?

What we have here then is a man *inexplicably* placed at the center of a network of iniquities, deprived of any efficacious assistance, and even of any consolation, having for his defense – with few exceptions nearly – some frightening men, enemies of Splendor as if they were demons, and identical, in their infamy, to the honorable outcasts who accuse him, and him not knowing what else to do, in his defense, than to cast, while groaning, a gloomy glance at the stupid ground!...

In his letters the absence of any religious feeling has been noted, the absence of any noble view as to the end of things, which is, one has to admit, quite frightening for an unfortunate man who fights against death.

In Rennes, he says: "Yes, my colonel! No, my colonel!" then he speaks about his wife while tears stream down his face. Ah! I know quite well that certain crybabies, to begin with myself, have difficulty resisting that. However, o Hebrew! if you were full of your father Abraham, if you were thinking on Moses and on the Prophets, if you believed in the Promise, you would have something to say to those generals, who are as imbecilic as they are vile, who would soil probably their medalled underpants... listening to you.

But you are a poor fellow in the shadows... you do not know anything.

Dreyfus then will be condemned, I dare predict, and divine Justice will not have received the slightest nick. He will be punished for an *unknown* crime – a rich crime – under the presumption of a known crime, which he appears absolutely innocent of and not responsible for. And this will be very fine. If God was not infallible, who would be?

As for what follows, I want to believe that my wishes should be fulfilled and that finally the definitive upheaval will be set in motion that I have so often announced.

September 8. – Yet another Danish person who speaks to me about the Affair! Occasion to remark, for the one-hundredth time, the immense interest of all foreigners in the Dreyfus case, and the universal, absolute scorn inspired by our Top Brass.

As I was writing the day before yesterday, it is too obvious for the least deep observer that the decision against this man is a foregone conclusion and that, for the whores in uniform who preside over the Court Martial, it is not a question, for one instant, of unraveling the truth, – which, besides, is known by everyone, – but simply and uniquely of unearthing a loophole in the condemnation that might not overly offend human conscience.

The unanimous feeling of foreigners is that this anticipated denouement would be, for France, a shame that it cannot recover from.

September 9. – "End of the fifth book" and... "*to be continued.*" Ah! that is a rude blow! Now, why should it finish? I ask you. How long will it continue, this nameless failure, which seems to the proud Cretin like a majestic river flowing?

This fifth book, which we have put behind us, ends naturally with the already-mentioned refrain (see August 13). But the curious thing is that it is intentional – that much is clear now – the characterization, the synthesis in that stupid rehash of his, in his own books, what he calls his work, his, Zola's. Seen in this light, the ritornello has something prodigious, and fantastic, about it:

"*... If one had* LAUGHED *less*, one would have heard the milk flowing, that little rivulet in the torrent of sap that rouses the world, that makes the great trees shiver in the powerful, July sun. Everywhere, fecund life charioted about the seeds, created, sired, nourished. And as for the eternal *labor of life*, the eternal river of milk flowed throughout the world."

O quibbling dozing men, o serene valetudinarians who liquify *silently* in the mechanical beds of Public Assistance, at the heart of asylums; – what do you think of this udder?

September 11. – One appears to have interrupted the massacre at the fecund man's place. Two cadavers sufficed. It was a trial, it was to test the waters. No longer finding in his imagination, which resembles that of a poet's as much as a peat bog does a lake, any avowable expedient to knock off the rest of his family, our author walks off as if nothing had happened. He moves on to something else. He shakes out the old fairground tent sheets of *l'Assommoir*, soiled with mud and bran, after twenty-five years, – and here we are again in a pretty world, at the home of a sex worker removed from the brothel, one does not know how or why, who practices virtue six days a week and rests on Sundays while working. Unfortunately, the Godless Pelagia did not foresee everything and allows herself be *beaten* by a "squat young man *of (sic)* brutal jaws," her son, alas! who was thrown into the garbage eighteen years earlier, the which son she had thought dead and whom she would voluntarily give one third of the skin off her back to make instantly disappear at the bottom of the dirtiest abyss.

The virtue of this sex worker is, according to the good old Cretin's thinking, something that ought finally to demonetize the dusty legends of Penitents and Virgins whom the Church honors on its altars.

September 12. – "The squat young man *of* brutal jaws" continues to *beat* his virtuous mother, who has no other recourse than the friendship of Mrs. Angelin (!), an old infecund woman tasked by Émile with supplanting advantageously the Little Sisters of the Poor who *have done their time*.[30] This lady, delegated by Public Assistance and not giving a damn – as seems appropriate – for the altogether Good God, pays a visit to the poor, "holding on her knees her little sack swollen with the gold pieces and silver pieces that she has to distribute."

There we have it, a thing that will surprise in-

---

[30]Original footnote: This expression is not Émile's. He is incapable of finding so original an expression.

discriminately all classes of society. The Public Assistance deducting some amount, were it but fifteen centimes out of the forty or fifty million a year divided among its mandarins, to *assist* indigents!...

Zola, naturally, falls for these jokes or if he does not fall for them, he feigns to fall for them, which is exactly the same thing for a nation, up until now French, that thinks that the New Testament was written, towards the middle of the XVIIIth century, by philosophers.

As for me, I have but one ambition left. I wait for the "Calvary," that of the virtuous sex worker, of course, who will be handed over to us soon, right, Lucien Descaves?[31] *At least I hope so*, as one of my former curates, speaking of the martyr, used to say, which he supposed rather unlikely for his flock and for himself.

I have already spoken of that rage for prostituting words. To be precise, the word *martyr* makes me think of the vile stupidities of the present moment. One is so deep into the flesh, and the abolition of the meaning of words is so demanded, that it is enough to speak of sufferings to awaken the idea of a Martyr. There are children martyrs, women martyrs, there are even animal martyrs. The meaning of the word is absolutely destroyed.

Those famished atheists who subsist exclusively on the scraps of ideas left by the Church on the golden table that all peoples have sat down to, and who lack even the intestinal gratitude of poor dogs, – see how they dishonor, how they ridicule, that unfortunate Dreyfus who ought to make them so full of

---

[31]Calvary... Lucien Descaves: this is likely a reference to the Naturalistic novel by Lucien Descaves, *Héloïse Pajadou's Calvary,* published in 1883.

pity! The only thing they can offer him, in his frightening misery, is the most stupid, the most repugnant of commonplaces:

> *"His children should know how much he suffered, how great a man he is. They should know that there is, always, an aureole around his head and that, from one end of Europe and the civilized world to the other, his name is discovered, like the name of the most NOBLE of martyrs, B. GUINAUDEAU." (l'Aurore, Sept. 10)*

Saint Etienne, Saint Laurent, Saint Georges, twenty million others who were the VOLUNTARY *Witnesses* of Our Lord Jesus Christ and, for that reason, called *Martyrs*, – where are you?

I just read the decision of condemnation, just today, for I am in Denmark. 5 for, 2 against. What are they doing here these two poor useless voices that would do so well asking for alms on the main highway to heaven?

While waiting for a more loudly implored "Calvary," I have the consolation of assisting at Dreyfus' "crucifixion" by Clémenceau. (*l'Aurore*, September 11) It is a shame, I can never say it enough times, to recur to such idiotic refrains, above all when one is a writer. But the nearness of Zola!...

September 13. – Have I mentioned that the Cretin, for several days now, has abandoned Balzac (*The Country Doctor, The Village Curate*) for Eugène Sue and that he seems to throw himself wholeheartedly on *The Mysteries of Paris*? (That is, the story of the assassination of the lady with the small sack by the Grenelle bandits.) He would plagiarize the most original works if he could recognize them. He will, I dare think, cut out several chapters from *Atala* or *Paul et Virginie*. Maybe even, around the 195ᵗʰ installment, he will discover a fable by La Fontaine as little known as the *The Cricket and the Ant*, or *The Funeral Oration of Mrs. Henriette*, because it has to do with striking while the iron is hot, to surprise people.

Ah! yes, I know it well, the end of ends would be to publish things that are completely and forever ignored by *his* readership, some pages by Barbey d'Aurevilly, for example, or Villiers de l'Isle-Adam, or Léon Bloy even. But for that, one would need, at least, to have heard of them. Then again, the readers of Urbain Gohier would no longer be there, and Zola himself would not understand a thing, his literature hardly surpassing night school.

O Ubu! once again, come to my aid.

September 14. – *The Fifth Act*, Émile Zola's article (*l'Aurore* of the 12ᵗʰ). "I am in a state of fright," he says, "... *sacred terror*." Last June there was *the little sacred lamp* (it also) carried by the same imbecile who seems to enjoy this phrase evidently. Sacred or not, Émile's terror consists above all in seeing France "roll into the abyss."

On the part of three or four guttersnipes who did the most, for so long, to topple this empress of nations, such a hypocritical word would already merit the most ignominious volley of slaps, while waiting for the last punishment. Today, however, it is so extraordinary that I remain dumbstruck.

One remembers the staggering article mentioned here, the 7ᵗʰ of June, when the "little lamp" was spoken about. Ah! well I believe that that there takes the cake. Without a doubt it is always a question of "sufferings" and of "despairs" in his "exile" unto himself, Zola. Without a doubt it is always spoken about when referring to this novelist of the drainpipe, exclusively and vindictively considered by himself as the Center and the Umbilicus.

But under the present circumstances the intensity, the violence, the flagrancy of Me appears to have something novel about it,... something of Barrès!...

That has a lot to do perhaps with the infinite absence, simultaneously stupefying and vomitive, of all talent for expression. Before becoming the Prince of prose writers, Émile was able, at a pinch, to commend himself for a static, disorderly prose that earned him the thumbs up of traveling salesmen and the majority of stationary shopkeepers; but since then, ah!, since then,... things have gone so horizontal that it is almost impossible for him to remain standing on his own two feet. Were he one hundred times the "good citizen" that this low villain claims to be, I know no human or divine clemency that could absolve the dirty low bastard of a writer for vilifying the French language to this extent!

Is it not stupefying? There is Dreyfus condemned, once again, in the most dishonorable fashion by the judges, and under circumstances that would have demanded effort to not aggravate the already unspeakable shame of our Military Command. Émile announces that he will speak, that same Émile already famous for a poorly-explained intervention, and who is certainly appalling for his reasons. Given he is, without contradiction, the lowest mind that has ever be seen, the multitude is with him, the world listens to him. What will he say?

Ah! nothing at all, other than that he is a "good citizen," a martyr, him too, a person coming back from a bitter "exile," a "patriot deprived of sleep" as long as the "truth is progressing"; finally, that he is "ready to pay," that precious truth, "with his freedom and with his blood." He does not say with his *money*, I beg the bad citizens to take note of it.

Four hundred fifty lines of commonplaces that a furious imitation of Clémenceau makes seem more ignoble is hard to swallow. "Special mentality... obscure mentality... Jesus was condemned once... The idea will be crucified, the saber must stay king..." etc. Finally, it appears that this is enough for a certain number of magnanimous people.

But the tone of this funny man speaking about the man whom he proclaims himself non-stop to be the defender and savior of, the tone of defamatory forgiveness and ignominious protection employed by the bastard speaking about the soldier! – this soldier, has he ever been more dishonored? – it is frightening. Shame and fear. "This pitiable Dreyfus, the poor human wreck who would make stones weep...", etc.

It is proper, however, to note that he names his involuntary client very infrequently, the 450 lines being, before everything and above all, for Émile Zola's benefit. Instead of the title: *The Fifth Act*, unintelligible in the Absolute, oh! and how! he should have entitled it bravely: *Me*! and have remained content, as his signature, with the last phrase mentioning something that comes *in a bolt of lightning* or *by thunderbolt*, I cannot remember.

September 16. – Zola, the people of *l'Aurore*, the adversaries of the people of *l'Aurore*, civilians and military men, judges and those subject to the law, witnesses and false witnesses, Catholics and Free Masons, Jews, Protestants, honest people! What a legion of riffraff! What an immense pile of idiots or bandits! What shame! What horror! What desolation!

Impossible to extract anything from this installment. It is too stupid and the language spoken in is too abject. One would need to cite the same inanities over and over again forever and a day. The only thing to point out is the more-than-crazy intent of the author to want to go on forever.

Why is that? Who can say? He has been paid, right, Vaughan? paid a lot. His kind of book is finished, for a long time now, so finished that it is no longer within the power, even of an angel, to understand anymore what is happening in it, for the conclusion of this work, filthy but arch-deranged, was, *from the beginning*, like the end of a visit to the brothel is, in its fat gilded issue. And then what? He tried do as Balzac did and that did not work out. He tried to do as Eugène Sue did and that failed immediately. Now he tries one does not know what. He tugs behind himself lamentably, here and there, his port-a-potty. Why does someone not put this poor old man out of his misery?

September 17. – I would like Urbain Gohier to make me a gift of his portrait. I visualize him quite clearly as one of those incorruptible shoemakers from 1793 whose *tongue* disgusted Napoleon. Nonetheless, maybe he would not have refused the beauty and elegance of a male hairdresser. Morally and politically, these two aspects do not lack confluence.

"The military profession," he writes, "is, principally, the school of cowardice." (*l'Aurore*, September 14.) Of course, it will not be easy to say that I wallow in the upper echelons of the Top Brass.

Mercier's or Major Carrière's stupid and venomous gobs, for example, if I had been imposed on to contemplate them forever, it would have seemed like a very strict purgatory. But this unbridled flunkey who dares claim that the soldiers of the Republic and the Empire, – without aiming too high – were *cowards*!... It is like asking if the chroniclers of *l'Aurore*, whose ambitions tend I know not where, are not *intentionally* Dreyfus' worst enemies and most cruel assassins.

Come on! what does one expect a good but uninformed, or perhaps very informed, officer to think, reading such a phrase to Philippeville, Pointe-à-Pitre, or Chambéry? He will naturally, invincibly think that one is correct to say that there is a conspiracy against the army and that those gentlemen's Dreyfus, even supposing him innocent of the crime of treason, is, all the same, in their hands, a pretext and an instrument.

"This sinister mannequin," the oracular Clémenceau writes, that very same day, twenty centimeters away from Urbain. Bizarre and inhuman declaration! One's jaw drops when one reads these things!

Have you read the genealogical chapters in Genesis, the Paralipomenon, or Ezra? Ah well! take a look, if you want to know what our Cretin has undertaken, in chapter 11, book six, of *Fecundity*. There was nobody to oversee him at that moment. He counts off, *by calling them by their names*, the children, grandchildren, and great grandchildren of the fecund man. It is unheard of, enough to put you away, enough to make elephants explode!

September 20. – Spent the day reading in part the collection of issues of *The Cross* dealing with the Affair. Horrible sadness and disgust. I do not know what revolts me more, the incomparable villainy of these religious flunkeys, always on the side of the man they judge to be the strongest – or the surprising baseness of their thought.

Oh! those minds of a seminarist, never departing from the shameful inanity of a frightening puerility, if for no other reason than to fill up on excremental pleasantries that have, in their eyes, this advantage of not offending "holy virtue."

Certainly! Émile's whoring turpitudes are delicate, madrigalesque, refreshing, lily-like, virginal, in comparison.

Some ecclesiastics, otherwise correct, one wants to believe, who reject with indignity, with horror, a book by Balzac and who would expurgate Ezekiel, do not consider themselves impure by lending an ear to chamberpot stories or by speaking, with what finesse! about M. Labori's "BULLET HOLE"!!! (*The Cross*, August 24, 1st page; August 26, supplement; September 16, 2nd page).

On August 26, there was the song that follows, played to the tune of the *Casquette* evidently:

THE SONG

From the "Attempt on a Man who Carried Himself Well."

It appears that last week
A well-known Dreyfusard
Like General Brugère
Received some lead in... his *back*.

Have you seen

The bullet hole, the bullet hole
      Have you seen
The bullet hole in Labori.

All the gendarmerie
Look for the unknown assassin,
Who had the barbarity
To wound a man in... the *back*.

      Have you seen, etc.

The lawyer survived
His terrible wound
Although it was very hard
To get a bullet in the... *back*.

      Have you seen, etc.

One hastens to have the eminent
Dr. Reclus extract it;
Seconded by a colleague
He performs a search in... the *back*.

      Have you seen, etc.

Mr. Doyen runs to the rescue,
But... *trala la la la*
The wounded man, who was scared stiff,
Didn't want to show him his... *back*.

      Have you seen, etc.

In brief, after so much suffering,
The lawyer returned to take
His place in the courtroom

While keeping the bullet in... his *back*.

Have you seen, etc.

He gives a pretty harangue
His glibness has returned
There's nothing unties the tongue so much
As having a bullet in... the *back*.

Have you seen, etc.

From deep within the recesses of my Danish
fjord, I hear bursts of laughter and unbounded joy by
ten thousand country or village curates, reading this
filth to their vicars, while returning from church
where they recited, after communion under both
species of the Eucharist, – and God knows with what
feeling! – the priest's sweet prayer:
   Corpus tuum, Domine, quod sumpsi, et San-
guis quem potavi, adhereat visceribus meis et præsta,
ut in me non remaneat scelerum macula, quem pura
et sancta refecerunt sacramenta...
   It is useless, I think, to recall that these charming things are written under the Image of Our Cruci-
fied Lord, who, for twenty years now, is seen on the
first page of *The Cross*, and whom one is sure to find
in all public or private latrines.
   Certain houses called *Missions*, in Copenha-
gen and throughout all Lutheran Scandinavia, provide
for their clients small copies of the *New Testament*,
on pious tables, in those places of necessity. But what
is that, compared to the permanent profanation – by
Saint Augustine's children! – of the adorable Sign?

September 21. – I learn that Dreyfus was pardoned. Boy was he lucky, that guy! one might say. I would like to be pardoned myself. On this subject, M. de Pressensé[32] wrote a few words that trouble me like a rhinoceros over a clarinet.

It is said that, little satisfied with a denouement that does not reinstate him, that Israelite now wants to go after those who calumniated and persecuted him. We will never get out of the labyrinth of that *honor*.

If the unfortunate man was a Christian and a real man – I have already said something along these lines – he would go, starting today, into *voluntary* solitude which he would fill with his silence and prayer, in this way making use of, with his eyes focused on death, the unordinary suffering that his miserable friends so stupidly call his *martyrdom*.

September 24. – Émile asks me why I speak so little about his installment, these last few days. What can I say to this poor fellow, other than that I have run out of strength and expedients? Nothing to harvest.

Today, however, there appears to be a semblance of something. Let's see. There is an old idiot accountant, naturally commended by the author who does not hesitate to make him destiny's prey. Why and how does this inoffensive man, having turned ferocious, end up wanting to turn everything upside down? By what sophism, moreover, can they be explained, I do not say his passions, but his simple passionate desires in a mastic society deprived of the appearance even of life and which peels off, every day, in the hands of an impoverished glazier who consid-

---

[32]Francis de Pressensé: a journalist and political figure who supported Émile Zola in the Dreyfus Affair.

ers himself, at minimum, Michelangelo's equal?

Apart from the hysterical need to make it last until the end of the world, if that were possible, a work that was finished before it began, I can find no excuse for the supererogatory adventures that the pitiable Émile wants to paste, using I do not know what horrible mucus, to the superabundant and loose leaves of an impossible episodic novel, already in transit to every grocery store in the two hemispheres.

But let us not get off topic. I spoke of a semblance of something. Here it is: After the death of the old accountant who dies while killing I do not know whom or I do not know what, one finds, at his home, on a table, "as if on an altar of religious offering" – before the photographs of his wife and his daughter who were murdered twenty years earlier by abortionists – "more than one hundred thousand francs of gold, silver, and even copper coin."

For a quarter of a century, he ate only stale bread and lived like an indigent, offering all that he earned to those ghosts.

It is clear that Zola who calls this "a bouquet" and who is compelled, in effect, to represent to himself a religious cult only under monetary species, must have, necessarily, stolen this story from some poor defenseless devil, and did not understand a word of it. It adds absolutely nothing, to be honest, to his installment save a little more confusion and obscurity. But one catches a glimpse of what it could have become under the quill of another writer.

And now we find ourselves at installment number 125. That makes about seven hundred pages, and *nothing has been said yet*. It has been noted, in recent years, that these unreadable ball-less works get longer and longer. One has no idea when they will end. In the present case, even if it means I should be skinned alive, I am forced to declare that on the seven-hundredth page, the Cretin's novel gives the impression of just getting started. There are people, very similar to beasts, who have worked, fornicated, for thirty years, to build a sublime family of granite. One could believe that is that. Not at all. It already begins to show cracks on every side. The seven hundred pages would therefore be merely a kind of prologue!...

Ah! in this case, I am done with it. For more than four months I have gargled, each morning, with this elixir of decrepitude, this rejuvenating water of the grave. It is too much to ask of a poor father with a family.

It is enough to make one turn into a tapir, always reading the same syllables deprived of meaning, strung together to create the semblance of words that are always predictable and the shadow of phrases that are absolutely identical: "the faith in life... the hope in life... an attempt on life... the flowering of goodness, joy and vigor..." There is an old, highly-appreciated sot who "succeeds at living in the serene gaiety of his hope in life"!... It is incredible the stupidities and filth that men can be made to swallow, when they are given the gospel of the non-existence of God and universal whoredom.

A dirty trick to play on Zola would be to ask him what he means by LIFE. But what is the point? His response would not be even remotely interesting.

The poor man who has never been conscious of the least rudiment of philosophy and who must think that the word *Metaphysical* belongs to a forgotten language from the Stone Age would be astonished like the first shopkeeper to come along that one should ask him about so simple a thing.

He responded with affability, – all the while tearing up a new sheet of paper, – that life consists in earning money, eating well, sleeping well, making love well, and defecating well. What other response is to be expected from such a mind?

September 25. – *Letter to Mrs. Alfred Dreyfus by Émile Zola*

Five hundred lines to tell this lady that her husband is a *martyr* and that he, Zola, another martyr, is, moreover, a POET. But what kind of martyr and what kind of poet? You will see soon enough.

This letter written "despite the citizen's mourning, despite the indignant grief, the revolt where just souls[33] continue to anguish themselves," (*sic*) is written "under the lamp," in "the brothel" (!!!) to the wife of the "martyr", the "crucified," the "re-suscitated deceased having returned alive and freed from the tomb."

The sender "saw only one thing," and that was that "an innocent was suffering," and I give you my word that he knows what it means to be innocent and to suffer! Then, naturally, he did everything. "How many times, for two cruel years, these two last years of *giant battles*, I have despaired of having him re-turned alive to his family!... An affair of the heart! My God! yes, my heart alone was taken."

Finally God, the "*great God*" so often and so piously invoked, has had the goodness to stir. "The torture victim has descended from the cross,... the nails are removed, and the martyr," covered with "spit," wet with "bile and vinegar"... and he has come

---

[33]Original footnote: He did not dare write *souls of the just*.

to sit "under the light of the familial lamp."[34]

Now what happens? This martyr, this cruci-fied man who is quite certainly "the most innocent among innocents, before all the peoples of the earth," this "hero greater than others, because he has suffered more..."(???), this Dreyfus decidedly, "becomes *God*."

And here is this:

"We erect an altar for him in our heart, having nothing more *pure* nor *precious* to give to him...."

The heart of Zola!... An altar in the heart of Zola!!!

And now, peoples, listen to this:

It is at the foot of this altar, and nowhere else, where "the triumphal acquittal, the resounding repara-tion" will take place and where "*all generations* on their KNEES" will be seen, "in memory of the glorious torture victim, asking pardon for their fathers' crime."

Is that it? No, there is something more beauti-ful yet.

"Here, Madam, we arrive at the summit. There is no higher glory, there is no higher exaltation... This innocent man, look at him there, having become the symbol of human solidarity, from one end of the earth to the other. While the religion of Christ had taken four centuries to *be formulated* (?????), to conquer *some* nations, the religion of the innocent man, twice-condemned, has gone *around the world,* at the drop of a hat, reuniting in an immense unanimity all civilized nations. I search, throughout the course of history, for a similar movement of universal brotherhood and I

---

[34]Original footnote: This locution, quite frequently used, it is said, among merchants of lorgnettes, reappeared many times, without verifiable utility. It is an exquisite attention to detail than anyone other than Émile would have cut.

cannot find it."

It is the same way for original expressions and new ideas. Poor Émile really is unlucky.

"For *the first time*, in history, all humanity gave a cry of liberation." He still lacks the cheek to write about *redemption*, but only by a small hair.

"And may he be honored therefore, may he be venerated, the man elected by his suffering, *in whom universal communion has just been taken.*"

Ah! well, yes, I have to confess, I like "the bullet hole in Labori" much better, it is less stupid.

As for "around the world," what can I do, in all fairness, other than throw myself behind the rabbit of a man who tells me that the best religion is the one that goes around the world the quickest?

That, for example, is rich, I have to confess. Only, I am a bit confused. Émile had already proposed to us the religion of *work*, then the religion of *life*. Today, it is the religion of Dreyfus. Which of these goes the quickest? What is the best brand? Everything depends on it. Ah! how convenient it is and how beautiful to be dealing with apostles who think!

And now without leaving the luminous perimeter of the "familial lamp," would it not be appropriate to speak a little about the Poet?

"It is we, the Poets, who give glory, and it is we, still, Madam, we, the Poets, who nail the guilty to the eternal pillory."

We, of course, means Zola all by himself. It would be crazy to suppose that this personal pronoun implied, for example, Urbain Gohier, Cyvoct, Lucien Descaves, or Mrs. Paule Mink.

Think on it, that here is a poet, a true poet, who works naturally for "forty years," yes, Madam, who *suffers* for "forty years," who is a martyr himself and who, by consequence, has the right to say some-thing, right? Ah! well, this poet whom human insults cannot touch, tells you that everything is okay and that, moreover, he is there, HIM, you understand this, Madam, that HE is there, asking you to sit down "un-der the familial lamp" with the martyr. That will make two of you, "under the lamp," which is the poet. Which is not banal, certainly. There you have it.

September 29. – I confessed, several days ago, that things were not going so well anymore for the fe-cund man. Ah! well, suddenly, things have sorted themselves out. Why and how? One will never know. Unexpectedly, it so happens that with a new install-ment, everyone is in the process of embracing and shedding tears of joy. As it turns out everyone has made a fortune. One of the fecund man's children has become a king of industry; another, a king of trade or of the *central* bank, I do not remember which; yet an-other, the king of flour, and of the flour mill; another, finally, the king of Africa... etc., etc. Ah! clearly who then, in France, at the present moment, would still keep the antique traditions of *royalty* if not some characters in a novel whom the All Powerful has birthed, around the time of Paul Bourget, in order to clean the chamberpots and wipe mud off the shoes, – but who left that bushel shining on the chandelier?[35]

The father had only to stamp his foot on arid ground to transform it into a paradise. Everything these people touch is a success, so that in truth the most ample benediction, previously thought to be the exclusive share of the friends of God, is today the rec-ompense of families who procreate after the manner

---

[35]bushel shining: clearly a reference to the parable of the lamp under a bushel in the New Testament.

of rabbits or arachnids.

But, at this moment, the installment is finished, arch-finished, over-finished, ultra-finished. All
has been demonstrated and proven, the economic and
patriotic urgency to multiply the children of others, to
raise them like swine, as well as the surprising imbe-
cility of a scribe deliquescing over the years.

Alas! no, it is not finished.

September 30. – My faith! it is true. There is
still the *diamond jubilee of marriage* which I had not
foreseen, but which was completely indispensable for
displaying and enumerating – as always in the manner
of *Genesis* – the fecund couple's "pullulating lin-
eage." Now Matthew is ninety years old and Marianne is eighty-seven. Their spawn, their happy milt,
all "that tide of girls and boys, that they left behind,
previously, to *flow freely* with their love, with their
faith in life," are now totaling THREE HUNDRED individuals raised, it goes without saying, on the same
dungheap as their parents; and one has, what is more,
the advantage of finding oneself in an absolutely *unknown* epoch.

That there is one of the Cretin's great ideas.
Think on it, that at about the time when this multipli-
cation began, there were already bicycles!...[36] Sixty or
eighty years have passed, which puts us in the second
half of the next century. One would love it if Émile,
soliciting his own genius, could shed a little light on
this future for us.

Only, then as now, – if one knows anything,
one knows, at least, this – the poor man is excluded
from all marriage ceremonies. On this point, Émile
has never varied, and will never vary. Émile does not

---

[36]bicycles: bicycles were invented in the early 19th century.

like it that one should be without money.

Every time the poor man appears in one of his agreeable books, he is to be dishonored, reviled, massacred, as in *l'Assommoir* or *Germinal*.

This filthy Italian idiot's hatred of the Poor has no equal except the instinct of idolatrous domesticity wherewith he throws himself at the feet of all simulacra of Wealth. Then, only, does it get fired up, what he dares monstrously to call his heart.

October 6. – Where are we now? What has become of the feast of the diamond jubilee of marriage? We had left three hundred individuals at the table, swarming progeny of the fecund couple. You would think, perhaps, that that was enough. Ah! well, no, there is a surprise.

What do we behold, suddenly, but a young man who appears, who calls himself "son of the good Niger itself, of the miraculous fecundity of its waters." He does not forget to add that this river, – which he appears to confuse with the Mississippi or the Amazon – "is immense and gentle, that it rolls out innumerable waves, like a sea... that not one bridge spans it, that it fills the horizon from one end to the other, that it has archipelagos and squadrons of enormous fish, etc. that it is, like the Nile, the father of countless generations, the creator God of a world still unknown which, later, will enrich old Europe... And the Niger valley, the good giant's colossal daughter, ah! *what pure immensity!*... etc., the plain, the fields, the furrows in a straight line, as far as the eye can see, which the plow would take *months* to reach the end of... the leagues of labor, *rolling with eternal harvests.*"

All in all, life in a republic, in other words,

Cockaigne,[37] nothing more.

"One does not even have to work. It is enough to scratch the earth with sticks. Miraculous hunting and fishing... Black lions, eagles, hippopotamuses that *resemble black babies*!!! On the day we possess agricultural machines, we will need flotillas of boats to send the overflowing abundance of our granaries to you..." Pointless to talk about other riches that are innumerable.

One says that Christopher Columbus sought terrestrial Paradise in the Antilles. Zola, does even better, he finds it in the Sudan.

"Finally, we are pastors, we have flocks, ceaselessly *being reborn*, to the point that we cannot keep an accurate headcount. Our goats, our sheep with their long wool, are by the thousands, our horses gallop freely in parks large as cities, our bison cover a league of river banks, where they descend to drink from the Nile..." The donkeys, or rather, the pigs of the motherland, with or without humps on their back, whether they drink or not, would cover assuredly a much vaster expanse.

Such is the "France of tomorrow," if one wants to believe it. Ah! without a doubt, there are some obstacles. Algeria will not be connected to Timbuktu starting tomorrow morning. Perhaps not even after five hundred years. No problem. "We will teem there and we will fill the earth... Come with me then, as you are too crammed together. (One would think he is speaking to herrings.) I have room for you all, I take men, I take women... etc., etc., etc."

---

[37]Cockaigne: an imaginary land of plenty and comfort, formulated in the Middle Ages. Anything that a peasant might dream of having – abundant food, sex, money... is there for the asking or the taking.

I beg your pardon for these imbecilic citations, but it seemed to me useful and even... patriotic to denounce an ADVERTISEMENT that recalls so well those torrents of gold that were made to flow before the eyes of Panamanian investors. – Free of charge, doubtless, Zola being even stupider than he is a rogue. But capitalists, small or great, must always be protected. Are they not the little intestines of France?

After all this lyricism about remote stuff, what is left is this, that the talkative young man is the son of the man who is one of the sons of the breeder who just conquered Africa. This conqueror, who does not seem to be just twiddling his thumbs, has had *eighteen* children, and the current clown has four himself already. In twenty years time, there will be six hundred of them perhaps. Behold what it means to *have faith in life*. One has children and bisons beyond counting. One has also the Niger river and its archipelagos. Until the unknown man who becomes fecund. "The unknown man's seed being sown, it could produce a harvest of fabulous potency."

Is there any reason to mention that all this happens *"cheerfully,* under the blistering sun in the tropics"?

With that, the old fecund female ancestor rises, with just enough time to renew her litter: "To the health of those who will love, she says, who will give birth, who *will create the most life*!!!" This decrepit butt is persuaded, by her faith in Émile, that one CREATES life.

The gala ends, there is a last triumph around the very old fecund couple. "It was the tide of victorious fecundity that seized them with joy... Them, in their old age, in the DIVINE STATE OF CHILDHOOD that they returned to, they did not always recognize the little boys or girls... Then, there were the mothers in the process of breastfeeding, who gave breast, while seated under the trees, enjoying each others' company, their tongues loosened, in proud serenity. It was the *decisive victory of fecund maternity over virginity, which kills life*."

Then, the refrain again:

"The milk flows non-stop from nourishing bosoms, eternal sap of living humanity. And this river of milk carried life along through the veins of the world, and it swelled, and it overflowed, for infinite centuries."

Idiot.

October 7. – The *last* installment of "Fecundity" is brought to me at last. God be praised for ever and ever!

Some citations:

"The more *life* possible, for the more happiness possible. Such was the *act of faith in life*." One million francs, I offer one million francs to whomsoever can explain to me the meaning of those words.

"Not one step forward has been taken in History, except that it was the *masses* that set humanity moving forward."

There have never been *great men*, guardians of the people – prior to Émile. That is well understood. One believes, at Médan, that Caesar is an Assyrian word that means *multitude*. It is admirable how base ideas come into this literary tinker's head who is accustomed to bawling about his industry in the poor quarters!

"Obligatory work. It is incorrect to say that it is imposed on men as a kind of punishment for their sins... It is, on the contrary, the *very soul of the world*

(???). Let the children grow, they will be instruments of wealth." Thus speak in whispers, when they still have the semblance of a soul, the slave traders.

"And it is *life* again that will have conquered, the renaissance of honored, adored *life*; this renaissance of the *religion of life*, crushed down under the long, execrable nightmare of Catholicism."

The cult of the future, it is "the fecund woman and the fecund earth." There you go. In each city or village, two temples: the Temple of Work and the Temple of Sex. Around the first, instead of the ordinary boutiques of objects of piety, there are merchants of cudgels, whips, riding crops, spurs, halters, bullwhips, etc. In the vicinity of the second, a humble commerce of hygienic sponges, bidets, douches, toilet paper, condoms even, in general all the accessories that a sage, albeit ardent, piety might desire. This will be a great deal nicer, in fact, than Christianity, – is that not right, Francis de Pressensé?

"Matthew and Marianne wind up as *life's heroes*. And, in their grandeur as heroes, there was also all the desire with which they had burned, the divine desire, fabricator and regulator of the world that had visited them in *bursts of flame*." Ah! that feels good to run into it again, one last time, that good old acquaintance of a phrase!

It appears that the two old people think a lot about the cemetery, where their innumerable children accompany, doubtless, with joy, those so very tenacious senile folk. "They hope to lie down there together, on the same day, for they cannot conceive *life* (!) without one another." Did I hear that correctly, Lord? Are these two mummies going to make more children, in their grave?...

What can really be at the bottom of the intimate thought of this miserable mind, of this harmful transcriber of commonplaces, of this imbecile, that is enough to make a grown man cry? It seems to me that the word *life* which is encountered on almost every line of this last installment and which fills the entire novel, could be the key to the puzzle.

Here I ask pardon of Christians, of all categories of Christian, from the heroic types, if there are any still alive, – but they have better things to do than read me – to the pudgy types and pachydermoids. There are, I know, rapprochements of ideas that are horrible, and combinations of words that resemble blasphemies.

However, the truth must be spoken.

Now, we know, from the Gospel, that it is Jesus who is the Life, and that it is he himself who teaches us this: *Ego sum vita.*[38] All Christianity is right there for the capable intelligences of the Absolute.

Of course, it would be indescribably outrageous to the agile and incandescent Spirits of heaven, for even one moment, to ascribe to Zola a like intelligence. But without understanding, he was able to read or heard that Christians believed this; he was able to see there, with his large, unintelligent eyes, a sort of pious formula that he had the means to make use of, while profaning it, while letting it rot, like a desperate flower in the frightening mud of his entrails. It is well known, moreover, that an instinct coming from Below always warns, infallibly, of those servants of the Devil.

At that moment appears a stupefying and, above all, incomprehensible phraseology, as long as the idea of *sacrilege* by abuse of the Word does not

---

[38]*Ego sum vita*: Latin for "I am the life."

present itself to the mind.

In this way, and only in this way, can the assemblage of words, otherwise so stupid, be explained, such as: "the faith in *life*... the victory of *life*,... the *religion of Life... life's* heroes,... *life* demanding heroism,... insatiable *life* that wants *everything* to be given to it,"... and, to conclude, "the city of peace, truth and justice," that is to say, "the only desirable reign of *sovereign* LIFE, mistress finally of time and space"...

Replace the word "life" by the terrible Name, *in quo omne genu flectatur cœlestium, terrestrium et infernorum*[39], and see if this does not cause fear!...

I am told that a Belgian who was extremely taken up with the Cretin's works, resolved, one day, to pay him a visit.

Unable to contain himself, he rushes off to Paris, then to Médan, and, on the verge of ringing at the gate of that disgraceful house that resembles a novel from the series, he notices all of a sudden a serious man, in suspenders, whose austere face was furrowed with innumerable wrinkles,... in the act of vomiting from a window above or from a balcony.

"Who is that pig?" asked this child of the Meuse, of a peasant.

"That is Monsieur Zola," responded the rustic. What a revelation contained in this story!

Have I said all there is to say about this unfortunate man who is about to die, without knowing that he was an imbecile for forty years and a criminal for forty years? Maybe. However I would not want to go away without having given him an alms.

My poor Émile.

---

[39]*in quo... infernorum*: Latin for "before whom every knee is bent, in heaven, on earth and in hell," scil., God.

You must leave us then!...

Nothing good, alas! can be thought nor even supposed of an individual such as yourself who never had a noble thought nor a generous act. Remember your ocean of filth... As far as Dreyfus is concerned, how can you possibly presume the disinterestedness of a lawyer who had so much to gain and so little to lose?

Does not everyone know, for a generation and a half now, that you are an indescribable villain, infinitely difficult to classify and completely unmentionable? Jules Barbey d'Aurevilly, the superlative artist who so obstinately refused to let you so much as scrub his floor, said it much too often to be ignored. What can I do?

If I speak to you, Zola, if I find the strength to surmount the horrible disgust that you inspire in me, it is because I think, all the same, about your poor soul.

You absolutely want people to admire you for having defended that captain, for having *accused* – others!...

Oh! the sad vision that visited me, in the humble church in Kolding, while observing the Stations of the Cross, at the very moment when I was praying before a barbarous image of the XIIth station!

Someone who has the misfortune reading you and whom I do not wish to name, had expressed to me, a few days ago, the most haughty disdain for the individuals – unworthy of all interest – your books have been able to sully, that is to say, fundamentally, disdain for the little people, the poor, the weak, the vanquished, the crushed. "What does it matter," he wrote to me, "next to such a great role he's played and when he has such a powerful lever (the quill of the author of *J'accuse*, of course), what does the imbecilic novel *Fecundity* even matter?"

That disdainful man, who is one of the most recent and deplorable conquests of that Alexander of shopkeepers, affected me deeply, has passed into a dark furrow of my memory. And, at the same time, at the same second, without my prayer being bothered by it, I believed I could see the *crushed* people of today, on the island of the Abyss, held there by spiritual chains stronger than iron, sequestered in an infernal deprivation of hope, and whose *trials* could not, must never, be revised by any man.

The name of the *Shopkeeper* of that nightmare was Émile Zola. He earned four hundred thousand francs a year to sell death, and had never given a *sou* to anyone. In consequence, many millions of sots and rogues considered him on a par with a very great man, and he smeared excrement at his leisure on a people, who were otherwise Christian, whom God's justice had put on earth.

So, once again, I think that the height of stupidity is to believe that you could be magnanimous, for even one hour, that you could do something generous. Your nation is not like that, your apostate and degenerate nation. If you appeared to perform an honest act, it is because you had or believed you had an interest in performing it, – even if that interest could only be made manifest on the Last Day.

Let's see, old fondler of the Third Estate, old stimulator of the phallus of a patented people, confess that you remember the article you published in the *Figaro*, on January 18, 1896, and that you entitled: "The Solitary Man." This solitary man, it is you, the man however of herds, of multitudes, but you hardly see the logic. Shakespeare earned very little money

and Dante even less. You are therefore much superior
to them. There, that is what we are to understand. The
article, moreover, was horribly written.

Admit it, you still have that same cataplasm
over what stands in for your heart. Yes, without a
doubt, I take it you suffer for being thought of, by
young people – perhaps also by some old people like
myself – as a good-for-nothing nincompoop and senile old man. Your Venetian probity forced you, in
the said article, to strum that guitar indecorously. It
was impossible for you to hide that you bawled while
dribbling at the mere thought that young men, – who
read passionately the poor poets like Barbey d'Aurevilly, Villiers de l'Isle-Adam, and Paul Verlaine, –
considered you to be an old trowel smearing shit. Was
it my fault? I ask you.

You needed, at any price, a revenge, and the
Dreyfus affair, happily, presented itself. *"At your
great age, in the* STATE OF DIVINE INFANCY *to which you
returned,"* it was quite natural for you to want to appear a hero. So you defended, *saved* Dreyfus who is,
now, a leper to you and who would prefer his Devil's
Island, if he only knew you.

In my opinion, the most authentic crime,
atoned for by the most infamous expiation, is preferable to your averred innocence. But here is something
that will make the constellations turn their croups and
run:

The author of *Earth* and so many other pieces
of filth, has become the avenger of oppressed Innocence! the demander of Justice!! the witness of
Truth!!!

There you have it, the last shame; there you
have it, the last insult for France!

Long live the dead!

France was drunk with military glory, since Napoleon above all. The war of 1870 sobered it up in a terrible way. Something, however, remains of that former drunkenness. The renewal of the great Emperor's glory, in his last years, quite proves it.

One demonstrates, today, to this unlucky nation that its generals are brutes or villains, that its military greatness no longer exists... And behold France in despair!

What an opportunity for you, Émile! You did not miss it. One gives you credit for that.

But now, o miserable man, now that your grief, as a very low rogue, is conceded, today while the Occident with its Saints and Heroes lies in your garbage pale, do you really think that a thousand innocent galley slaves, rehabilitated by your dirty prose, could pardon you for this inexpressible profanation?

Listen, if you are capable of listening and understanding. You were born, one does not know where, as all who exist are born. So be it. It is said that you are of a Venetian backwater. I believe it. One is born where one can be, one is what God wills.

But to be, absolutely deprived of what is called, over the centuries, *the French spirit*; to be a fat ass, a congenital oaf, as incapable of putting a smile on another person's face as smoothing out the knitted brow on his own; and, at the same time,... reigning over France! that is what takes the cake. I have to admit.

Who would believe it, however? All that is not enough for you. You need the centuries to come. You have written to Mrs. Dreyfus that you were a POET and because of this a distant posterity would observe what you have left!...

How is it possible, my poor man, that you

have not one friend to inform you that in the hour following your death, probably as impending as it is ignominious, not one human being will be able to remember what you have or have not written; and that a little later still, as the buyers of your works disappear and the chamberpots themselves are discouraged by the immensity of your *bouillon*, – that you will become *very bad business*?

Sad Zola, nothing will remain for you but the Augustinian Fathers of the Assumption and their "bullet hole"![40]

Those fellows, I dare hope, will soon enough know what they owe you, and they will be perhaps, – having taken off, finally! their soutanes, – your last readers.

From here on out, Émile, you will no longer understand a word I am about to say. I leave you then and I will speak to others.

A more than human word might be necessary to appreciate sufficiently the sacerdotal abasement represented by those frightening religious. The recent scandal of the journal *The Cross,* to say nothing about other pious rags, is enough to nail the Savior back up on the cross.[41]

Modern ignorance and, above all, impiety, as one knows, is in large part due to viewing a Priest as a man. That is, I believe, the vilest idea of the century, the most universally advocated, by consequence. It

---

[40]Original footnote: See above... Same publishing house, *Pèlerin*, September 24. Cover story, the Image of Mary with these words above it: "Adveniat regnum tuum" and, on the back, a huge chamberpot. Father Bailly's idea.

[41]*The Cross*: a newspaper founded by the Augustinians of the Assumption. The paper was a leading voice against Dreyfus.

was inevitable then that the ravages of such a scene should be enormous for a people who had, for so many months, before their eyes the unspeakable spectacle of a group of priests coming down relentlessly on a poor man whose unjust condemnation they were *fully aware of,* – their mouth full of the Blood of Christ – as they licked the boots, splattered with blood, of his tormenters!

They are rare, today, the Christians who know that Christianity is *all about* the Sacerdocy!

I have a friend, a sort of mathematician who, by one of those miracles in which the understanding of men is disconcerted, was able to preserve a lively soul and an intelligence capable of a certain number of vibrations.[42] This wonderful man had written to me an insane letter informing me that after the inconceivable turpitude displayed by those religious who hope thereby to effect the end of an atheistic government, he no longer felt any need for the mediation of any priest between God and himself.

How many others like him whom I do not know! There is nothing to do about it evidently. The scandal created by those men who received the power to consecrate the Bread and the Wine and to expel demons is an incontestable scandal, a contamination that nothing can efface.

… But it would be delirious of me to try to instill in an end-of-the-century cranium the rudimentary evidence that mathematical certitude is not shaken by the indignity of a geometry or ten thousand geometries, and that it is outside the power of any bad priest to weaken or invalidate the authority of God's Commandments or the Church's Commandments.

---

[42]Original footnote: Do I need to say that this mathematician has since then severed all relations with me?

That exceeds a contemporary mind's capacity.

This Dreyfus affair, moreover, which I have spoken about with great reluctance, solely because of Zola, is, without question, one of the strangest in the world. I do not say the *greatest*, but the strangest.

Like other famous catastrophes, it served to *riddle* souls. A huge, appalling waste. One was aware of the infinite number of imbeciles, cowards, renegades, slaves, prostitutes, hangmen, and this number was equally divided *on both sides*.

As if something deep and completely innermost was in danger, – one saw multitudes lose their reason, not only in France, but in Europe and all over the globe. I am looking for a period of time in the past when the delirium, furious stupidity, and hypocritical ferocity of a lie had been more *universal*.

All this infinitely exceeds the Jewish captain and resembles the prodrome of the Cataclysm. Now that the filthy and stupid trial of Rennes is over, how can there be any doubt that the misfortune of that man had been a pretext for two kinds of dogs who are fighting over France tooth and nail.

The prisoner of Devil's Island – returned to his family and drinking milk now – is no longer of interest to anyone. Nobody speaks about him anymore. The war machine has stopped functioning, the tool or pawn has been put aside; but each troop of accursed men has maintained his position of combat, his line of battle.

And the total oblivion into which that unfortunate man's name which once deafened the earth, the sudden silence having come, after so enormous a clamor, has an unspeakable terror to it.

One awaits SOMEONE.

Post-Scriptum

Gentlemen of the Jury, you will not condemn Émile Zola. He is the honor of France. – M. Labori

# # #

This morning, October 14, I receive a copy of *Fecundity* which just came out. Enormous mass of 750 pages and 26,000 lines!!!

I learned then that this book is the first in a new series incredibly entitled:

THE FOUR GOSPELS

L'Aurore had not leaked a word of it. The Cretin wanted a surprise and, my faith! I had it – it was, for me, like a sock in the stomach. How to divine, in fact, that so rotten a writer might have such spirit?!!!

Everything is clear now, the choice of the name *Matthew* and the *genealogical* lists, probably also some other details, unintelligible as long as one is ignorant of the intentions of that exegete who knows barely how to read, whose ignorance is infinite and who understands the holy Text as well as an Italian cow can understand the Lord's Prayer.

It would evidently be of no interest to anyone to mention, one more time, the perfect impiety and, if I dare say so, the bad faith in impiety, of a scribe of the lowest rank whose every line is saturated, without his knowing it, with Christian references that were inculcated in him in his miserable first infancy, and who dares "speak of the execrable nightmare of Catholicism"!

Before exhaling something about the "martyr" captain, the ineloquent indignation of a paralytic; before slobbering, against this or that soldier, accusations of deceit, crime, or abuse of power; does not anyone think that this justicer of the toilet, this knight of evacuation, should have previously been exonerated for the shameful calumnies found in his cowardly novel on Lourdes and the low jibes in his pamphlet against Rome where he will never forgive any human being for having received him like a little shit?

But what can I say? For several lustra now, he writes, doubtless, *on command*, like those who acquit criminals or condemn the innocent. Occult societies affiliated with every demon that exists would be too sottish, really, not to make use of so perfect a slave!

Let us wait then for the three Gospels to appear. Émile gives himself thus, generously, three more years, at the very least.

Ernest Hello – whom he is, without a doubt, incapable of deciphering one line of and whose name he does not even recognize – has said several times, and in different ways, that when a man rejoices over himself, believing himself to have overcome fate, and when he summons Providence to appear before him, his death is near. Let us hope so!

To finish up with the *Four Gospels*, it is not difficult to predict that, with the protagonist of the first having been named Matthew, that of the second will be named Mark, that of the third Luke, and that of the forth John. This rudimentary idea is completely within Émile Zola's capacity.

But here is what troubles me. For Saint Luke and for Saint John, it follows of its own accord. Saint Luke will furnish him the occasion of a filthy blasphemy that one can guess at, which will infinitely please all traveling salesmen, and his glory will be incalculably augmented. Saint John will lend him his wings of an Eagle. One will learn decidedly that "the Word is in him, Zola, and that it is he who is the Word." It is very simple, as one can see.

As for Saint Mark, I do not know. I can only see the *Lion* as being of use to him. Still, one must know or remember that one day in the past, this poor polecat of an Émile referred to himself as a lion (*Gil Blas*, March 25, 1894).

In fact, what an opportunity it presents to continue the little advertisement for the Niger and the colonization of the Sudan, the which appears to be, in effect, a sacred country full of "black lions" and "bison"!

Honestly, this stinker could die tomorrow. God's grace is what is needed charitably to be wished for for the damned who can only increase anymore the inexpressible rigor of their eternal punishment.